BBC Micro Assembler Workshop

Bruce Smith

Shiva Publishing Limited

SHIVA PUBLISHING LIMITED
64 Welsh Row, Nantwich, Cheshire CW5 5ES, England

© Bruce Smith, 1984

ISBN 0 906812 67 4

An interface was used to produce this book from a microcomputer disc, which ensures direct reproduction of error-free program listings.

Typeset and printed by Devon Print Group, Exeter

Contents

Introduction

The *BBC Micro Assembler Workshop* is aimed at those of you who have been delving into the delights of the BBC Micro's excellent assembler. It is a natural progression from *BBC Micro Assembly Language*, but will be invaluable even if you learned assembler with any of the other assembly language books available for the BBC Micro. It provides a bench full of useful assembly language routines and utilities programs and examines the techniques involved.

An extensive use of vectored addresses is made throughout the Beeb's operation, allowing modifications to be made to the manner in which the micro operates. Chapter 2 begins by showing how one of these vectors, the command line interpreter vector (CLIV), can be caught to allow new RAM based commands to be added to the already extensive vocabulary of the Beeb. A short 'wedge' interpreter is provided and the techniques for adding your own commands examined. To get you going, six commands come supplied with the wedge interpreter: *BELL, *HOME, *ON, *OFF, *CLEAR and *GRAFRITE.

Chapter 3 looks into the causes of the 'Bad program' and uses the results to come up with the 'CURE'.

String manipulation is an important facet of any program handling strings of data, be it an adventure game or the latest stock control reports. Chapter 4 provides four assembler listings showing how character strings can be compared, copied, deleted and inserted. Similarly, programs handling large amounts of data will often require it to be sorted into order—Chapter 5 shows how a bubble sort will facilitate this.

Conversion between ASCII-based numerical character strings and their two byte binary equivalents and vice versa is not straight-forward. Suitable conversion routines are described fully in Chapters 6 and 7, and working conversion routines are listed. Chapter 8 examines the various ways in which textual material can be printed on to the screen and provides a novel printing subroutine.

With Chapter 9, we delve into the innards of the Beeb and come up with a routine that will list all the values assigned to BASIC's integer variables. Utilities to move, fill and produce a hex and ASCII dump of memory are examined in Chapter 10, and these could be added to the Machine Code Monitor provided within the pages of Chapter 11. Many other processors can produce operations that would enhance the 6502's operation set. A software stack implementation similar to that found on the 6809 processor is produced in Chapter 12, allowing up to eight registers to be pushed onto a memory-based stack. The combination of registers is determined by the bit pattern of a byte embedded in the code.

To complement the BASIC Assembler, Chapter 13 provides a full disassembler written in assembler, allowing the mysteries of the MOS and BASIC interpreter to be unravelled. Finally, for those of you developing your own sideways ROMs or RAM, a copier routine is included which will provide a fast, efficient method of downloading their contents into RAM ready for running so that programs are permanently on tap.

Explanations are provided for BASIC I and BASIC II and, while every routine will run on OS 1.0 or greater, most will run on OS 0.1.

A couple of thank-yous are in order. Firstly, to Tony Quinn, Editor of Acorn User, for bailing me out with the loan of an 'office' printer when mine needed major surgery, and secondly, to Keith Parish of the same establishment for coming up with the title of this book. Thanks!

Highbury, October 1984   Bruce Smith

1 Opening the Tool Box

The routines supplied in this book are designed to make your life that much easier when writing machine code. Quite often, after mastering the delights of the Beeb's assembler, frustration occurs because the techniques involved in, say, converting between ASCII characters and their equivalent binary values are not known. Nor are they readily available in a published form, so the painful process of sitting down armed with pencil and paper and working out the conversion by trial and error begins.

This is just one example of the type of assembler program you will find within these pages. No specific addresses are used (other than those relating to the user zero page RAM area), and so the routines are fully relocatable.

BASIC is used freely to demonstrate the machine code's operation—rather than repeating sections of assembler code, BASIC is often used instead to shorten the overall listing. It is left to you to add further sections of assembler from other programs within the book, or from your own resources. For example, the penultimate chapter provides a machine code disassembler which requires the input of the address from which the disassembly process is to begin. In the demonstration this is indicated by a one-line INPUT statement. However, in Chapter 6 there is a routine for inputting four ASCII hex characters and converting this 'string' into a two-byte binary number. This routine can be inserted into the disassembler program to go some way to making it a full machine code program available for *RUNning. This is just one example—you will no doubt come across others.

WRITING MACHINE CODE

You have an idea that you wish to convert into machine code—so what's the best way to go about it? First, make some brief notes about its operation: Will it use the screen? If so, in which mode?

3

Will it require the user to input values from the keyboard? If so, what keys do you use? What will the screen presentation look like? Will you want to use the sound commands?...and so on.

Once you have decided on the type of thing you want, try to put these ideas down in flowchart form. This need not be the conventional flowchart using boxes and diamonds—I find it just as easy to write each operation I want the program to perform in a list and then join the flow of these up afterwards.

Quite often, the next step is to write the program in BASIC! This may sound crazy, but it allows you to examine various aspects of the program's operation in more detail, an obvious example being that of obtaining the correct screen layout. You might find, after running the layout routine, that it does not look particularly good. Finding this out now will save you a lot of time later, avoiding the need to rewrite the screen layout portion of your assembler—rewriting BASIC is much simpler!

Try writing such a BASIC 'tester' as a series of procedures—this will make the machine code conversion process much easier. Let's consider the main loop of such a BASIC tester that takes the form:

```
PROC_set_variables

PROC_set_up_screen

REPEAT

PROC_input_values

PROC_convert_as_needed

PROC_display_values

PROC_update_values

UNTIL TRUE
```

Each module can be taken in turn, converted into assembler and tested. Debugging the assembler is made easier because the output from each module is already known from using the BASIC tester. The final main loop of the assembler should then look something like this:

```
JSR set_variables

JSR set_up_screen

.main_loop

JSR input_values

JSR convert_as_needed

JSR display_values
```

```
JSR update_values
BNE main_loop
```

You might be surprised to learn that this technique of testing machine code programs by first using BASIC is employed by many software houses the world over.

A SUBROUTINE LIBRARY

You will find that many of the routines herein make admirable additions to an assembler subroutine library. Let's look at a few ideas that will make such a library easy to use.

When writing assembler, storage space for addresses and calculations will obviously be required—how can we ensure that different subroutines do not use the same locations? The simple answer is that we cannot! However, we can make life very much easier by declaring each of these locations as a variable name at the beginning of the assembler text thus:

```
30   address=&70
40   value=&72
```

Now, if new assembler text is added that uses similar locations, all that needs to be changed is the value assigned to the particular variable name (or names). When the code is assembled, the variable names are evaluated and their assigned values compiled. Failure to use variable names in this manner can result in long-winded editing being required. For example, the assembler:

```
LDA address_high_byte
```

assembles the operand specified in the variable 'address_high_byte' defined earlier, say &70. Similarly:

```
LDA &70
```

assembles exactly the same operand. Consider what happens if we wish to change the memory location specified in the operand from &70 to &88. In the first instance, where we used a variable name, only the value assigned to address_high_byte needs to be altered. In the second instance, however, the entire assembler must be searched and all occurrences of &70 located and edited to the new value.

While on the subject of variable names, it is worth making a few points. Firstly, always use variable names that mean something to both you and anybody else examining your program. The variable name 'temporary_address_hold' has much more meaning than 'addr' or 'temp'. Secondly, variable names are much more prominent if you use upper case characters for the mnemonics and lower case for variable names. Use the join character '_' to separate words within the variable name—again, this makes the program more readable and you will reap the benefit if you need to debug it. All these comments also apply to the use of labels for the destination of branches or jumps. A properly selected label informs the reader of the purpose of the coding that follows.

All the programs in this book are fully commented. By that I mean that the operation of each mnemonic (or group of mnemonics) is given a concise description. I hope that by reading through these you will appreciate just how valuable they are. You may feel that you don't need to comment your own programs—you know exactly what they are doing, because you are writing them. However, if you try to come back to a program a month or two after it was written, you may be surprised just how little you remember.

DEBUGGING

Finally, a word or two about debugging programs that do not perform as you had hoped. If this happens to you, before pulling your hair out and throwing the latest copy of *Machine Code Nuclear Astrophysics Weekly* in the rubbish bin, a check of the following points may reveal the bug!

1. Check that your labels have all been declared and correctly assigned.
2. If you are not already doing so, use an OPT command that will report errors on the assembler's second pass.
3. If using two-pass assembly, check that the value of P% is declared *within* the FOR…NEXT loop.
4. Have you omitted the NEXT statement at the end of the assembler when using two-pass assembly? If you have, the second pass will not be performed.
5. Are all your immediate addressing modes prefixed by a hash (#) symbol? LDA &41 will load the accumulator with the contents of location &41—to load the accumulator with the ASCII code for 'A' you need LDA #&41.
6. Are all your hex addresses prefixed by an ampersand (&) symbol? LDA 70 will assemble, but the operand will not be the

same as that generated by LDA &7∅, as was originally intended.

7. Check that you have set or cleared the Carry flag before subtraction or addition.

8. My favourite now—ensure that you save the result of an addition or subtraction! The sequence:

```
        CLC
        LDA low
        ADC #1
        BCC over
        INC high
.over   RTS
```

is not much good if you don't save the result of the addition using:

```
        STA low
```

before the RTS!

9. If you have set P% to point above the top of your assembler text, make sure that the text has not grown upwards so that it occupies memory above this value, because assembling the text will corrupt your assembler—bad program!

If none of these errors is the cause of the problem, then I'm afraid you must put your thinking cap on. Well-commented assembler will make this debugging process very much easier.

2 BBC Command

One of the disadvantages of using random access memory-based machine code routines is that it is left to the programmer to remember where they reside. This is not really a problem if only one or two utilities are present; the problem occurs only when several routines are being used.

A simple way out is to define specific function keys to call particular routines (or groups of routines). This means, however, that the function keys are not all available for use from within the program you are developing. A better method is to incorporate the machine code routines into the vocabulary of your computer by giving them names, so that they can be called simply by entering the command name allocated to the particular routine.

The trick in adding new commands to the Beeb's lexicon is to get it to recognize them. If an unrecognized command is entered, the almost immediate response is 'Bad Command'. If you have sideways ROMs present in your micro, for example a Disc Filing System or Word Processor, you'll know that it is possible to add commands. Virtually all new commands offered by sideways ROMs are implemented as Operating System commands, in other words they are prefixed by an asterisk. Thus *LOAD, *SAVE and *CAT are actually part of the Machine Operating System (MOS) and not BASIC, which makes them available for use even if BASIC has been paged out by another ROM.

This gives a hint as to how our extra commands can be added. They must be implemented as OS commands and our machine code must have a small interpreter that catches the processor's attention as it hands control from the BASIC ROM to the MOS.

This transfer is effected through OSCLI, the Operating System Command Line Interpreter, located at &FFF7. Actually, this is simply a standard entry point that immediately performs an indirect jump through a vectored address located at &2Ø8 and &2Ø9—more affectionately known by its makers as CLIV (command line interpreter vector).

The address contained within CLIV may vary depending on the MOS issue—in the 1.2 MOS it is &DF89. By altering the contents of this vector we can make it point anywhere in the Beeb's memory map, and therefore directly to a RAM-based CLI. The CLI can then try to interpret the command. If it does not recognize it, control can then be passed to the MOS so that there is no effect on the standard OS commands, other than a very slight increase in operational time. This technique is often referred to as a 'wedge'.

Two important points should be made here regarding the method used for returning from machine code that has been entered in this way. Firstly, if the vector is intercepted as just described in order to execute a wedge code, and the code constituting the wedge is not executed (because the CLI did not recognize the command), all registers must be restored to their entry conditions and a direct JMP made to the normal vectored address. Secondly, if the wedge code is executed and does not need further processing by the MOS, or if the wedge is used to completely replace the standard coding, a simple RTS will suffice to return control and the registers need not be restored.

Program 1 gives the complete listing to add this intermediate interpreter plus five simple routines that provide the following commands and functions:

*BELL	: Issues a bleep on the internal speaker.
*HOME	: Homes text cursor to top right of screen.
*OFF	: Turns flashing text cursor off.
*ON	: Turns flashing text cursor back on.
*GRAFRITE	: Allows text to be printed at the graphics cursor.
*CLEAR	: Clears values of all integer variables A% to Z%.

Program 1

```
10   CLIV=!&208 AND &FFFF
20   ?&208=0 : ?&209=&C
30   accumulator=&70
40   XY_address=&71
50   execution=&80
60   oswrch=&FFEE
70   FOR PASS=0 TO 3 STEP 3
```

```
 8Ø      P%=&CØØ
 9Ø      [OPT PASS
1ØØ      STA accumulator        / save accumulator
11Ø      STX XY_address         / save low byte CLI address
12Ø      STY XY_address+1       / save high byte
13Ø      LDX #&FF               / set table index
14Ø      .loop
15Ø      LDY #&FF               / set memory index
16Ø      .inner
17Ø      INY : INX              / increment both indexes
18Ø      LDA table,X            / get byte from command table
19Ø      BEQ zero_byte          / branch if zero
2ØØ      CMP (XY_address),Y     / compare with OS command
21Ø      BEQ inner              / if similar check next bytes
22Ø      .again                 / move to next command in table
23Ø      INY : INX              / increment both indexes
24Ø      LDA table,X            / get byte from table
25Ø      BNE again              / until 'Ø' located
26Ø      INY : INX              / move past 'Ø'
27Ø      LDA table,X            / get next byte
28Ø      CMP #&FF               / is it STOP?
29Ø      BEQ exit               / yes, command not here
3ØØ      INY : INX              / increment indexes
31Ø      JMP loop               / repeat command look-up
32Ø      .exit
33Ø      LDA accumulator        / restore registers
34Ø      LDX XY_address
35Ø      LDY XY_address+1
36Ø      JMP CLIV               / and into MOS
37Ø      .zero_byte
38Ø      INY : INX              / increment indexes
39Ø      LDA table,X            / get byte
4ØØ      CMP #&FF               / is it STOP?
```

```
410     BEQ exit            / yes, go to MOS
420     STA execution       / otherwise store low byte address
430     INY : INX           / increment indexes
440     LDA table,X         / get high byte address
450     STA execution+1     / save it and
460     JMP (execution)     / jump to execution code
470
480     .bell               / entry for *BELL
490     LDA #7              / ASCII bell code
500     JMP oswrch          / 'print' it and RTS
510
520     .home               / entry for *HOME
530     LDA #30             / ASCII home character
540     JMP oswrch          / print it and RTS
550
560     .grafrite           / entry for *GRAFRITE
570     LDA #5              / print at graphics cursor
580     JMP oswrch          / print it and RTS
590
600     .off                / entry for *OFF
610     LDA #23             / perform the VDU command
620     JSR oswrch          / VDU 23,1,0,0,0,0,0,0,0,0
630     LDA #1
640     JSR oswrch
650     LDX #9
660     LDA #0
670     .off_loop
680     JSR oswrch
690     DEX
700     BNE off_loop
710     RTS
720
730     .on                 / entry for *ON
```

```
740     LDA #23              / perform the VDU command
750     JSR oswrch           / VDU 23,1,1,0,0,0,0,0,0,0
760     LDA#1
770     JSR oswrch
780     JSR oswrch
790     LDX #8
800     LDA #0
810     .on_loop
820     JSR oswrch
830     DEX
840     BNE on_loop
850     RTS
860
870     .clear               / entry for *CLEAR
880     LDX #100             / 100 bytes to do
890     LDA #0               / clear accumulator
900     .clear_loop
910     STA &404,X           / clear variable byte
920     DEX                  / decrement index
930     BPL clear_loop       / continue until done
940     RTS
950
960
970     .table               / command table start
980     EQUS "*BELL"
990     EQUB 0
1000    EQUB (bell MOD 256)
1010    EQUB (bell DIV 256)
1020    EQUS "*HOME"
1030    EQUB 0
1040    EQUB (home MOD 256)
1050    EQUB (home DIV 256)
1060    EQUS "*GRAFRITE"
```

```
1070    EQUB 0
1080    EQUB (grafrite MOD 256)
1090    EQUB (grafrite DIV 256)
1100    EQUS "*OFF"
1110    EQUB 0
1120    EQUB (off MOD 256)
1130    EQUB (off DIV 256)
1140    EQUS "*ON"
1150    EQUB 0
1160    EQUB (on MOD 256)
1170    EQUB (on DIV 256)
1180    EQUS "*CLEAR"
1190    EQUB 0
1200    EQUB (clear MOD 256)
1210    EQUB (clear DIV 256)
1220    EQUB 0
1230    EQUB 255
1240    ]NEXT
1250 END
```

Before examining the interpretative part of the listing, look at lines
970 to 1230. These are responsible for constructing the command
table which the wedged CLI uses to see if the command it is
interpreting is in its newly extended dictionary. Figure 2.1 illustrates the structure of the command table in memory. Each entry
consists of three parts, namely:

1. The command name.
2. A zero byte.
3. The command execution address.

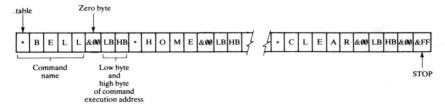

Figure 2.1   The command table structure

The command name is stored in ASCII format and this includes the asterisk. The zero byte indicates the end of the command table to the CLI, and the two-byte execution address is stored in standard 6502 format, low byte first. The very top of the command table is marked by a negative byte (&FF in this case), which I have termed 'STOP' to distinguish it from BASIC's TOP.

Compiling the command table has been accomplished using the psuedo-mnemonics EQUS and EQUB implemented on BASIC II. However, to keep on the good side of BASIC I owners, Program 1a gives the command table construction using string and byte indirection operators.

Program 1a

```
980    ]NEXT
990    $P%="*BELL"
1000   low_byte=(bell MOD 256)
1010   high_byte=(bell DIV 256)
1020   PROC_update
1030   $P%="*HOME"
1040   low_byte=(home MOD 256)
1050   high_byte=(home DIV 256)
1060   PROC_update
1070   $P%="*GRAFRITE"
1080   low_byte=(grafrite MOD 256)
1090   high_byte=(grafrite DIV 256)
1100   PROC_update
1110   $P%="*OFF"
1120   low_byte=(off MOD 256)
1130   high_byte=(off DIV 256)
1140   PROC_update
1150   $P%="*ON"
1160   low_byte=(on MOD 256)
1170   high_byte=(on DIV 256)
1180   PROC_update
1190   $P%="*CLEAR"
1200   low_byte=(clear MOD 256)
```

```
1210   high_byte=(clear DIV 256)
1220   PROC_update
1230   ?P%=0
1240   P%?1=255
1250   END
1260
1270   DEF PROC_update
1280   P%=P%+LEN($P%)
1290   ?P%=0
1300   P%?1=low_byte
1310   P%?2=high_byte
1320   P%=P%+3
1330   ENDPROC
```

Finding a place for the CLI and command table should not be too much of a problem. For purposes of demonstration I have assembled the entire code into the user defined character buffer located in block zero RAM from &C00 to &CFF inclusive. Although the command table is assembled directly above the CLI this need not be the rule, in fact, it can be placed anywhere in the memory map that is convenient.

Table 2.1 lists the details of the OSCLI routine entry and exit conditions.

Table 2.1   OSCLI details

OSCLI	Passes a text line to the Command Line Interpreter
Location	&FFF7
Vector	CLIV at &208
Entry details	X and Y registers point to command location in memory (X = low byte, Y = high byte)
Exit details	A, X and Y undefined C, N, V and Z flags undefined Interrupt status preserved

Figure 2.2 flowcharts the operation of the wedge CLI. Studying this should help you in your own understanding of the program's operation. The interpretative part of the listing is held between lines 100 and 460. As Table 2.1 shows, the two Index registers are used to

15

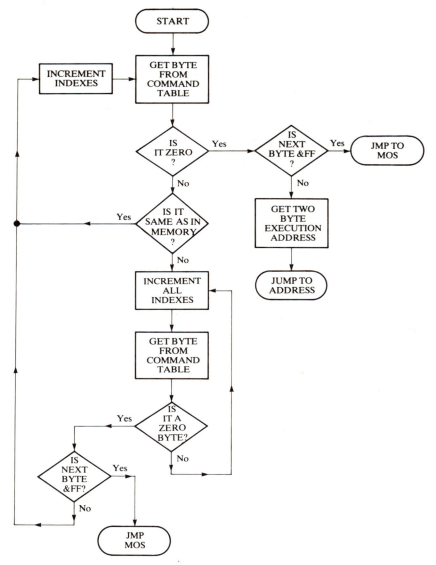

Figure 2.2   The wedge CLI flowchart

pass the address of the OS command to OSCLI—the new wedge
CLI must therefore preserve these two values in case the command
under scrutiny is not in the new dictionary. This is performed by
lines 100 to 120, the three registers being saved in the zero page user
area. For a final version wedge CLI this is probably not a good
procedure as it uses up precious zero page user space. The most
obvious alternative is to push them on to the hardware stack, or

16

they could be saved in a few bytes above the wedge CLI reserved specifically for this purpose. I have used zero page for the purposes of debugging, as it makes their values readily available to the '?' operator.

The two index registers are cleared (lines 130 and 150)—the X register is being used as an index to the command table and must therefore be initialized *outside* the main loop. The Y register is used as the index for post-indexed indirect addressing, thus allowing the program-based command table to be accessed.

The true interpretative part of the program commences in line 180 when an ASCII byte is taken from the command table and placed in the accumulator. If this is a zero byte, the Zero flag will be set and the branch of line 190 performed. Otherwise, the byte is compared with that held in memory. If the comparison succeeds, the loop is repeated and the next byte checked. It should be clear from this that if the OS command continues to match the one in the command table, this process will continue until the zero byte is reached. Assuming the command is identified, the branch to line 70 is effected. This extracts the byte following the zero byte to ensure that it is not STOP (generally, STOP will not be found once a command has been identified, but the check is included for expansion and safety reasons). The two bytes following the zero byte normally hold the execution address of the identified command, so these are loaded into a vector and an indirect jump made to the command coding, thereby allowing it to be executed. The RTS at the end of the command coding returns control back to the BASIC interpreter.

If, at any stage, the inner loop fails to identify a character, the loop is exited (line 220), and the zero byte at the end of the currently accessed command sought out. A check on the following byte is made to see if STOP has been reached. If not, the next command in the table is tested. If STOP has been reached, then the OS command was not part of the wedge CLI. In this case, the processor's registers are restored and the MOS entered via an indirect jump.

To implement the wedge CLI then, the CLIV must have its contents reset to point to it. This is handled by line 20. The low byte is poked into location &208 and the high byte into &209. Line 10 saves the normal CLIV address before this is changed so that the MOS can be entered at a later point if so required.

Important The following couple of points should be remembered. Firstly, if you relocate the wedge CLI in memory, remember to change the address bytes poked into CLIV by line 20. Secondly, always execute a BREAK and OLD before running the program, to ensure that the default value of CLIV is restored, otherwise the correct value will not be inserted into the variable CLIV by line 10.

THE NEW COMMANDS

Once the machine code has been assembled, the new commands are directly available for use. They may be used in the usual manner for OS commands, either in programs or directly from the keyboard in immediate mode. Just as with other OS commands, when used in programs they should be on a line by themselves or be the last command in a multi-statement line.

Executing *BELL at the keyboard will produce a bleep on the internal keyboard identical to that obtained with CTRL-G. *HOME prints an ASCII 30 code, which repositions the text cursor to the top of the screen without affecting any text on the screen. *OFF and *ON turn the flashing text cursor off and on. This is useful in many applications as the cursor can be somewhat annoying.

*GRAFRITE allows text to be printed at the current position of the graphics cursor, as the following short program demonstrates:

Program 2

```
10  REM ** *GRAFRITE DEMO **
20  MODE 5
30  DRAW 100,300
40  *GRAFRITE
50  PRINT"TEXT AT THE GRAPHICS CURSOR!"
```

The final command, *CLEAR, is perhaps the most useful of the bunch, as it enables the value of all the integer variables (A% to Z%) to be cleared. Although BASIC performs this task as part of its 'power-on' system initialization, there are times during a program's flow when it is desirable to reset variables. Chapter 9 contains details about the way in which these variables are stored in memory, and the following program prints their current values:

Program 3

```
10  REM ** PRINT VALUES OF VARIABLES A% TO Z% **
20  @ %=0
```

```
30   ?&70=ASC("A")
40   FOR loop=&404 TO (&404 + 100) STEP 4
50   PRINT CHR$(?&70);"%=&";~!loop
60   ?&70=?&70+1
70   NEXT loop
```

Typing *CLEAR (or inserting it in the program as line 80) and then rerunning the program will show that all the variables have indeed been cleared.

3   Bad Program Cure

The most frustrating message that can ever be produced by a BBC Micro is the ubiquitous 'Bad Program'. I'm sure most, if not all, Beeb users will have experienced this awful aspect of the Beeb's operation—perhaps after trying to reload a program from cassette or disc, or straight after RUNning a lengthy typed in program. Suffer no more! CURE, even if it does not restore your Bad Program to its pristine condition, will at least make it list, so that surgery under keyboard control can be performed. Bad Programs are a thing of the past!

Program 4

```
 10   REM ** BAD PROGRAM CURE **
 20   memory_address=&70
 30   line_address=&72
 40   line_length=&74
 50   CLS
 60   PRINT''''''''
 70   FOR PASS=0 TO 1
 80     P%=&7C00
 90     [OPT 0
100     .start
110     LDA &18              / get page value
120     STA memory_address + 1   / save
130     LDA #0               / low byte page start
140     STA memory_address   / save it
150     TAY                  / clear accumulator
```

```
160    LDA #13                      / get ASCII RETURN
                                       character
170    STA (memory_address),Y       / place at PAGE
180    .outer
190    JSR update                   / increment vectored
                                       addresses
200    LDY #0                       / reset Y
210    LDA (memory_address),Y       / get byte from memory
220    CMP #&FF                     / is it TOP?
230    BNE over                     / no, branch
240    RTS                          / yes, all done!
250    .over
260    LDA memory_address           / copy current memory
270    STA line_address             / address to start of
280    LDA memory_address + 1       / current line address
290    STA line_address + 1
300    JSR update                   / move vectored addresses
310    JSR update                   / on two bytes
320    LDA #3                       / point to line length byte
330    STA line_length
340    .inner
350    JSR update                   / increment vectored
                                       addresses
360    INC line_length              / and line length counter
370    LDA (memory_address),Y       / get byte from line
380    CMP #13                      / is it an ASCII RETURN
                                       character?
390    BEQ carriage_return          / yes, handle it
400    CMP #&20                     / is it less than 32?
410    BCS inner                    / no, branch
420    LDA #ASC' || '               / yes, illegal control code
430    STA (memory_address),Y       / replace with a ' || '
440    JMP inner                    / repeat inner loop
450    .carriage_return
460    LDA line_length              / get length of line
```

```
470   LDY #2                       / point to length in line
480   CMP (line_address),Y         / are they the same?
490   BEQ outer                    / yes, skip over
500   STA (line_address),Y         / no, store new value
510   BNE outer                    / start new line
520   .update
530   CLC                          / add one to both
540   LDA memory_address           / vectored addresses
550   ADC #1
560   STA memory_address
570   LDA memory_address + 1
580   ADC #0
590   STA memory_address + 1
600   RTS
610   ]NEXT
620   *SAVE"CURE" 7C00 7C5C 7C00
```

A better appreciation of the program's operation can be gained if you understand how a program is represented internally. Figure 3.1 illustrates graphically how a typical program is stored—in this instance it is the two lines:

```
10   PRINT "SARAH"
20   END
```

A BASIC line of text can be divided into two halves. The head of the line consists of four bytes. The first byte is always an ASCII RETURN character (&0D or 13). The next two bytes contain the line number stored in binary form, low byte first. Thus, line 10 is stored as &000A, line 20 as &0014, and so on. The fourth byte represents the length, in bytes, of that line. Looking at Figure 3.1 the line length byte is &0E or 14 decimal. The length is calculated from the start of the line, that is the low byte of the line number, to the termination of that line or the RETURN character. As only a single byte is allocated for holding the line length, BASIC lines may not exceed 256 characters in length (including the RETURN).

The rest of the line, its body, contains the actual commands, statements and text. In line 10 of the program example this is &20, an ASCII space, followed by the BASIC token for PRINT (&F1), another space and then the ASCII characters for ",S,A,R,A,H, and ''. Line 2Ø follows a similar vein, but its RETURN character is followed by &FF. This is the byte that the Beeb uses to mark the top of a program (in fact the value given to TOP is the address of the byte immediately after this). The reason for using this particular byte is that it is a 'negative' byte in signed binary form—it has its most significant bit set. It is because the Beeb uses this pseudo-negative line number to indicate the end of a program, that line numbers greater than 32,767 (&7FFF) are not acceptable. (32,768 (&8ØØØ) has its most significant bit set and this is allocated to TOP.)

PAGE

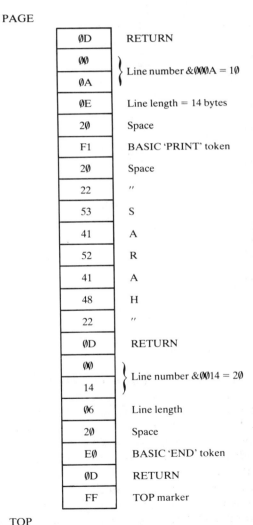

ØD	RETURN
ØØ	} Line number &ØØØA = 1Ø
ØA	
ØE	Line length = 14 bytes
2Ø	Space
F1	BASIC 'PRINT' token
2Ø	Space
22	''
53	S
41	A
52	R
41	A
48	H
22	''
ØD	RETURN
ØØ	} Line number &ØØ14 = 2Ø
14	
Ø6	Line length
2Ø	Space
EØ	BASIC 'END' token
ØD	RETURN
FF	TOP marker

TOP

Figure 3.1   Internal storage of program

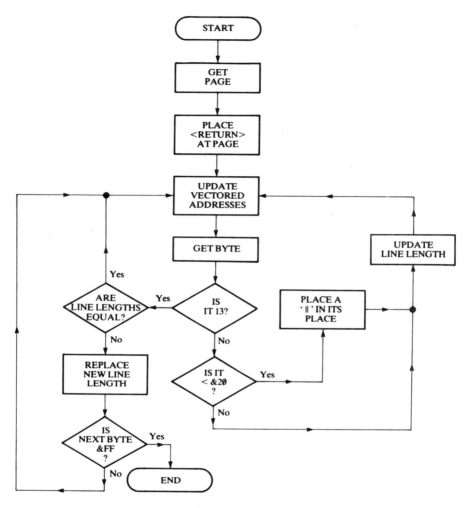

Figure 3.2   CURE flowchart

When a program is loaded into memory from a filing system, or is waiting to be run, BASIC checks through it to see that everything is in order, and to set the value of TOP so that it knows where to place dynamic variables and strings. As it works along each line it counts the number of bytes in each and then compares this with the line length byte. Nine times out of ten this comparison succeeds, but occasionally it fails, causing the dreaded error message, and preventing the program from being listed.

CURE operates by checking through the program resident at PAGE, counting each line length and resetting the line length byte if it is incorrect. The program also checks for any control code characters that may have become embedded, replacing them with || (ASCII 124) so that they can be edited out after listing, using the COPY and cursor control keys.

Once you have entered the program, recheck it thoroughly and then place a cassette into your tape deck (or a disc into the currently selected drive). This is necessary because line 620 will *SAVE the assembled program straight away.

You may have noted from line 80 that the machine code is assembled directly into the screen memory. This is a crafty but neat way of storing 'once-off' programs. Problems could arise for example, if you assembled and saved the code from &C00, then later you required the help of a CURE, but didn't want to destroy the contents of the user defined character buffer. Using the screen storage technique avoids this dilemma. When you assemble the code, don't be put off by the various bits of garbage appearing at the top of the screen—it's the machine code itself!

Lines 50 and 60 of the program are imperative when using this technique, to clear the screen memory and then to move the text cursor down several rows, thereby avoiding its corruption by any filing system messages that are issued.

4 String Manipulation

In this chapter we will look at the way in which ASCII character strings can be manipulated using machine code routines to perform the following operations:

1. Compare two strings.
2. Concatenate one string on to another.
3. Copy a substring from within a main string.
4. Insert a substring into a main string.

These types of routines are essential if you intend to write any programs that manipulate data and information. Adventure games are a typical example.

COMPARING STRINGS

String comparison is normally performed after the computer user has input some information from the keyboard. In BASIC this might be written as:

        100   First$="Move Left"

        110   INPUT"Which direction?" Direction$

        120   IF First$=Direction$ THEN PRINT "Correct!"

We do not always wish to test for equality, though. In BASIC, we are able to test for unlike items using the NOT operators '< >'. Thus, line 110 could have been written as:

        110   IF First$ < > Direction$ PRINT "Wrong!"

At other times, we may wish to test which of two strings has a greater length, and this is possible in BASIC using the LEN statement:

210   IF LEN(First$) >LEN (Direction$) THEN PRINT "First"
ELSE PRINT "Direction"

Program 5 gives the Assembler and BASIC listing for the string comparison routine, which puts all the functions described above at your disposal whenever the program is used. The Status register holds the answers in the Zero and Carry flags. The Zero flag is used to signal equality: if it is set (Z = 1) the two strings compared were identical; if it is cleared (Z = 0) they were dissimilar.

The Carry flag returns information about ths length of the two strings: if it is set (C = 1), either they were identical in length or the first string was the longer. The actual indication required here is evaluated in conjunction with the Zero flag. If Z = 0 and C = 1 then a longer string rather than an equal-length string is indicated. If the Carry flag is returned clear (C = 0) then the second string was longer than the first.

Program 5

```
10   REM ** STRING COMPARISON ROUTINE **
20   first_string=&70
30   second_string=&72
40   length_first=&74
50   length_second=&75
60   FOR pass=0 TO 3 STEP 3
70     P%=&C00
80     [OPT pass
90     .string_comparison
100    LDA length_first        / get length of first string
110    CMP length_second       / is it same length as second
                                   string?
120    BCC compare_string      / no, it's longer, so branch
130    LDX length_second       / yes, so get length of second
                                   string
140    .compare_string
150    BEQ condition_flags     / if zero branch
```

27

```
160    LDY #0                    / initialize index
170    .compare_bytes
180    LDA (first_string),Y      / get character from first string
190    CMP (second_string),Y     / compare to character in second
                                    string
200    BNE finish                / if dissimilar, finish
210    INY                       / increment index
220    DEX                       / decrement string counter
230    BNE compare_bytes         / branch back and repeat
240    .condition_flags
250    LDA length_first          / get length first string
260    CMP length_second         / compare length second string
270    .finish
280    RTS
290    .test
300    JSR string_comparison     / compare strings
310    PHP                       / push status on to stack
320    PLA                       / pull into accumulator
330    AND #3                    / save Z and C
340    STA &76                   / save flags
350    RTS
360    ] NEXT pass
370  INPUT"FIRST STRING :" FIRST$
380  INPUT"SECOND STRING :" SECOND$
390  FIRST%=LEN(FIRST$)
400  SECOND%=LEN(SECOND$)
410  $&4000=FIRST$
420  $&4100=SECOND$
430  !first_string=&4000
440  !second_string=&4100
450  ?length_first=FIRST%
460  ?length_second=SECOND%
470  CALL test
480  PRINT"RESULT :";?&76
```

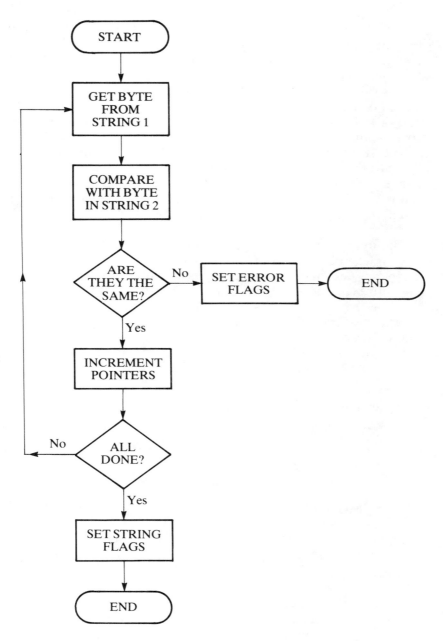

Figure 4.1   Compare strings flowchart

Once run, the BASIC text in lines 370 to 460 calls for two strings to be input. These are stored in memory from &4000 and &4100. The routine cannot handle strings greater than 256 characters in length (though it could of course be expanded to do so). The length of each string is also required by the routine, so this is ascertained and stored in the appropriate zero page bytes at &74 and &75 (lines 40 and 50). To allow the string buffers to be fully relocatable, the string addresses are held in two zero page vectors (lines 20 and 30).

The string comparison proper starts by evaluating the length bytes to find out if the strings are the same length. If they are not equal, then the strings cannot be identical. However, as the routine returns information on the string lengths it is still completed—the program compares bytes throughout the length of the shorter string.

The byte comparison is performed by lines 180 and 190 using post-indexed indirect addressing. When the first non-equal characters are detected, the main loop is exited to 'finish'. Assuming the entire comparison works, and the X register (which holds the working string length) has been decremented to zero, the length bytes (lines 250 and 260) are compared to condition the Zero and Carry flags before the routine completes.

The short test routine returns the Zero and Carry flag values and prints them out, indicating the following results:

Returned	Z	C	Result
0	0	0	Strings < > and string 1 larger
1	0	1	Strings < > and string 2 larger
3	1	1	Strings =

STRINGS UNITE

Strings may be joined together by a process called 'concatenation'. In BASIC the addition operator '+' performs this function. Thus the program:

```
100   First$="REM"
110   Second$="ARK"
120   Final$=First$+Second$
```

assigns the string "REMARK" to the string indirection operator called 'Final'. If line 120 were rewritten as:

```
120   Final$=Second$+First$
```

the resultant value assigned to Final$ would be "ARKREM". We can see from this that one string is simply tagged on to the end of the other, overwriting the former's RETURN character, but preserving the latter's.

This process of concatenation can be performed quite readily, as Program 6 illustrates. However, the actual BASIC equivalent of the operation we are performing here is:

First$=First$+Second$

In other words, we are adding the second string on to the first string and not summing the two to give a separate final string, though this is possible with slight modifications to the assembler text.

Program 6

```
 10   REM ** STRING CONCATENATION **
 20   first_string=&70
 30   second_string=&72
 40   length_first_string=&75
 50   length_second_string=&76
 60   index_first_string=&77
 70   index_second_string=&78
 80   count=&79
 90   overflow=&7A
100   FOR pass=0 TO 3 STEP 3
110     P%=&C00
120     [OPT pass
130     .string_concatenation
140     LDA length_first_string     / get first string length
150     STA index_first_string      / save in string one's index
160     LDA #0                      / clear accumulator
170     STA index_second_string     / set string two's index to zero
180     CLC                         / clear Carry flag
190     LDA length_second_string    / get second string length
200     ADC length_first_string     / add it to the first
210     BCS too_long                / branch if total > 255
```

220	JMP good_length	/ otherwise jump to good_length
230	.too_long	
240	LDA #&FF	/ load accumulator with 255
250	STA overflow	/ and store to indicate overflow
260	SEC	/ set Carry flag and subtract
270	SBC length_first_string	/ string one's length from maximum length
280	BCC finished	/ finish if first string > 255
290	STA count	/ save current count
300	LDA #&FF	/ restore maximum length
310	STA length_first_string	/ store in string one's length
320	JMP concatenation	/ jump to concatenation routine
330	.good_length	
340	STA length_first_string	/ save accumulator in string one's length
350	LDA #0	/ load with 0 to clear
360	STA overflow	/ overflow indicator
370	LDA length_second_string	/ get string two's length
380	STA count	/ save in count
390	.concatenation	
400	LDA count	/ get count value
410	BEQ finished	/ if zero then finish
420	.loop	
430	LDY index_second_string	/ get index for string two
440	LDA (second_string),Y	/ and get character from second string
450	LDY index_first_string	/ get string one's index
460	STA(first_string),Y	/ and place character into first string
470	INC index_first_string	/ increment first string's index
480	INC index_second_string	/ increment second string's index
490	DEC count	/ decrement count

```
500    BNE loop                    / repeat until count=0
510    .finished
520    LDY length_first_string     / get final length of first string
530    LDA #13                     / ASCII RETURN
540    STA (first_string),Y        / place at end of string
550    LDA overflow                / get overflow indicator
560    ROR A                       / and move it into Carry flag
570    RTS
580    ] NEXT pass
590    CLS
600    INPUT"FIRST STRING :"FIRST$
610    INPUT"SECOND STRING :"SECOND$
620    FIRST%=LEN(FIRST$)
630    SECOND%=LEN(SECOND$)
640    $&4100=SECOND$
650    $&4000=FIRST$
660    !first_string=&4000
670    !second_string=&4100
680    ?length_first_string=FIRST%
690    ?length_second_string=SECOND%
700    CALL string_concatenation
710    PRINT
720    PRINT"FINAL STRING IS :";
730    PRINT$&4000
```

This program allows a final string of 256 characters in length to be manipulated. Therefore, as the program stands, the combined lengths of the two strings should not exceed this length. If they do, then only as many characters as space allows will be concatenated on to the first string, leaving the second string truncated. The Carry flag is used to signal if any truncation has taken place, being set if it has, and cleared otherwise. As with the string comparison routine, the string buffers are accessed via two zero page vectors (lines 20 and 30), and two bytes are reserved to hold the length of each string. A further two bytes are used to save index values (lines 40 to 70).

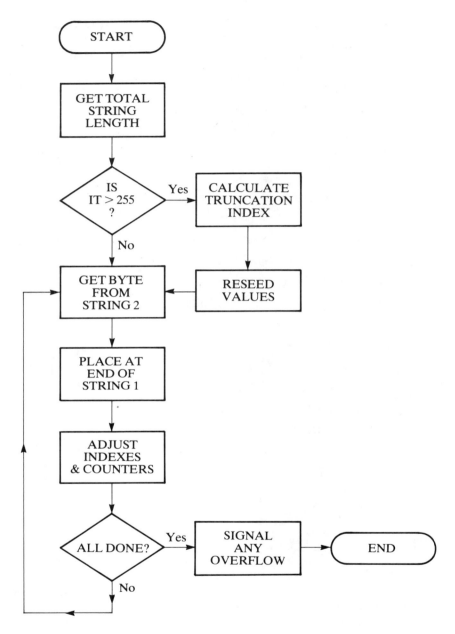

Figure 4.2   Concatenate strings flowchart

The first nine machine code operations (lines 140 to 220) determine the final length of the string by adding the length of the first string to that of the second string. A sum greater than 256 is signalled in the Carry flag. When this is set, the branch of line 210 is performed, the length of the first string buffer is set to the maximum (256) and the overflow indicator is loaded with &FF to show that truncation will occur.

The concatenating loop is held between lines 420 to 500. This simply moves one byte from the vectored address plus the index_second_string, and places it at the end of the first string, as indicated by the index_first_string byte. This process is repeated until the value of 'count' has reached zero. Lines 520 and 530 place a RETURN character at the termination of the string to facilitate printing from BASIC or machine code. The Overflow flag is loaded into the accumulator and bit 7 rotated across into the Carry flag, thereby signalling whether truncation has occurred.

COPY CAT

String manipulation routines must include a method of copying substrings from anywhere within a string of characters. In BASIC, three such commands are provided. They are MID$, LEFT$ and RIGHT$, although with the first of these, any point in a string can be accessed. The following shows the sort of thing possible in BASIC:

```
100   Main$="CONCATENATE"
110   Sub$=MID$(Main$,0,3)
120   PRINT Sub$
```

Running this will output the string "CON". What it has done is to take the three characters from the first character in the Main$. Program 7 produces the same type of operation from machine code.

Program 7

```
10   REM ** COPY SUBSTRING FROM STRING **
20   source_string=&70
30   substring=&72
40   length_substring=&74
50   length_source_string=&75
```

```
 6Ø    count=&76
 7Ø    string_index=&77
 8Ø    error_flag=&78
 9Ø    FOR PASS=Ø TO 3 STEP 3
1ØØ        P%=&CØØ
11Ø        [OPT PASS
12Ø        .copy_substring_from_string
13Ø        LDY #Ø                          / initialize Y
14Ø        STY length_substring            / clear byte
15Ø        STY error_flag                  / and error flag
16Ø        LDA count                       / get substring length
17Ø        BEQ finish                      / if null string, finish
18Ø        LDA length_source_string        / get string length
19Ø        CMP string_index                / compare with index
2ØØ        BCC error                       / error if index is greater
21Ø        CLC                             / clear Carry flag
22Ø        LDA string_index                / get index
23Ø        ADC count                       / add substring length
24Ø        BCS truncation                  / branch if > 255
25Ø        TAX                             / move index across
26Ø        DEX                             / decrement it
27Ø        CPX length_source_string        / compare with string length
28Ø        BCC greater_or_equal            / branch if string length
29Ø        BEQ greater_or_equal            / is > or = to the index
3ØØ        .truncation                     / return as many characters as
                                             possible
31Ø        SEC                             / set Carry flag
32Ø        LDA length_source_string        / get string length
33Ø        SBC string_index                / subtract the index value
34Ø        STA count                       / save new length
35Ø        INC count                       / and increment it
36Ø        LDA #&FF                        / denote an error by
37Ø        STA error_flag                  / setting error flag
38Ø        .greater_or_equal
```

390	LDA count	/ get length
400	CMP #&FF	/ compare with maximum length
410	BCC copy_substring	/ branch if count is
420	BEQ copy_substring	/ < or = to maximum length
430	LDA #&FF	/ maximum length
440	STA count	/ store in count
450	STA error_flag	/ and also in error flag
460	.copy_substring	
470	LDX count	/ get index position
480	BEQ error	/ error if zero
490	LDA #0	/ load accumulator with 0
500	STA length_substring	/ clear substring length
510	.loop	
520	LDY string_index	/ get index
530	LDA (source_string),Y	/ get character from main string
540	LDY length_substring	/ get substring index
550	STA (substring),Y	/ copy character into substring
560	INC string_index	/ increment index
570	INC length_substring	/ and substring length
580	DEX	/ decrement count
590	BNE loop	/ loop if not zero
600	DEC length_substring	/ decrement final length
610	LDA error_flag	/ get error flag
620	BNE error	/ error if flag set
630	.finish	
640	CLC	/ no error, clear carry
650	BCC out	/ and finish
660	.error	
670	SEC	/ error, so set carry
680	.out	
690	LDA #13	/ ASCII RETURN
700	LDY length_substring	/ get substring length

```
710     INY                          / move index past last byte
720     STA (substring),Y            / place RETURN there
730     RTS
740     ] NEXT PASS
750     !source_string=&4000
760     !substring=&4100
770     INPUT"SOURCE STRING "source$
780     source%=LEN(source$)
790     ?length_source_string=source%
800     $&4000=source$
810     INPUT"STRING INDEX "mid%
820     INPUT"STRING LENGTH "len%
830     ?count=len%
840     ?string_index=mid%
850     CALL copy_substring_from_string
860     PRINT$&4100
```

Once again a few lines of BASIC demonstrate the operation of the
routine, requesting the source string, starting index and length of
substring, or rather the number of bytes to be copied into the
substring from the starting index. The main string is in a buffer
located at &4000 and the substring is copied to its own buffer at
&4100. As always, these addresses may be changed to suit user
needs as they are vectored through zero page (lines 20 and 30).

Error-checking is allowed as the Carry flag is set on exit if an
error has occurred. Normally, an error will occur only if the starting
index is beyond the length of the source string, or the number of
bytes to be copied from the main string is zero. If the number of
bytes to be copied exceeds the number left from the indexed
position to the end of the string, then only the bytes available will
be copied to the substring buffer.

On entry to the routine, error-checking is performed (lines 160
to 240) and if any errors are found the program exits. Lines 300 to
370 perform a truncation if the number of bytes to be copied
exceeds those available. The copy_substring loop (lines 510 to 590)
copies each string byte from the vectored address in the main string
to the substring buffer. Each time a character is copied the substring length byte is incremented. On completion of this loop,
controlled by the X register, the error flag is restored and the Carry
flag conditioned accordingly (lines 610 to 680). Finally (lines 690 to

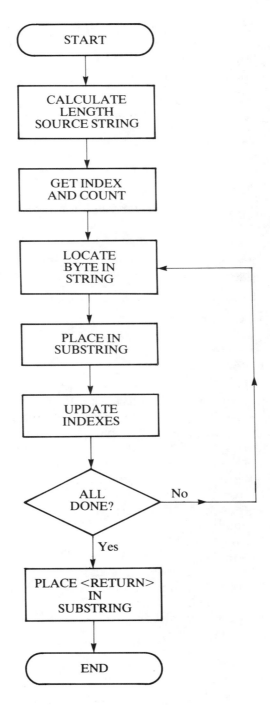

Figure 4.3   Copy string flowchart

73Ø), an ASCII RETURN character is deposited at the end of the substring.

The following example shows the resultant substrings produced from the main string "CONCATENATE" for different indexes:

Index	Length	Substring
Ø	3	CON
3	3	CAT
4	3	ATE

Figure 4.4 illustrates the index value for each of the main string's characters.

String	C	O	N	C	A	T	E	N	A	T	E
Index	Ø	1	2	3	4	5	6	7	8	9	1Ø

Figure 4.4   String Index

INSERTION

This final routine provides the facility for inserting a string within the body of another string, allowing textual material—for example, in word processing applications—to be manipulated. If the main string held 'Elizabeth okay', calling this routine to insert the string 'rules' would produce a final string 'Elizabeth rules okay'. As with the COPY routine, the position of the insertion is pointed to by an index byte and the Carry flag is set if an error is detected—that is, an index of Ø or a null substring is specified. The maximum length of the final string is 256 characters. If the insertion of the substring causes this length to be exceeded, the substring is truncated to the length given by (256 minus length of main string) and only these characters are inserted.

Again, a BASIC primer demonstrates the use of the routine. The string buffers are held at &3ØØØ and &31ØØ and in this instance they are accessed directly, although there is no reason why vectored addresses could not be used.

Program 8

```
1Ø   REM ** INSERT ONE ASCII STRING **
2Ø   REM ** INTO ANOTHER ASCII STRING **
```

```
 30   main_string=&3000
 40   sub_string=&3100
 50   string_length=&70
 60   substring_length=&71
 70   offset=&72
 80   source=&73
 90   destination=&74
100   error_flag=&75
110   FOR pass=0 TO 3 STEP 3
120   P%=&C00
130   [OPT pass
140   .add_string
150   LDY #0                    / clear Y
160   STY error_flag            / clear error flag
170   LDA substring_length      / get substring's length
180   BNE zero_length           / branch if non-existent
190   JMP good                  / otherwise carry on
200   .zero_length
210   LDA offset                / get offset
220   BEQ error                 / error if non-existent
230   .check
240   CLC                       / clear carry
250   LDA substring_length      / get substring's length
260   ADC string_length         / add to main string's length
270   BCS cut_off               / branch if over 256 bytes
280   CMP #&FF                  / maximum length
290   BEQ calc_length           / branch if = or <
300   BCC calc_length
310   .cut_off
320   LDA #&FF                  / maximum length
330   SEC                       / set carry
340   SBC string_length         / subtract length
350   BEQ error                 / branch if total
```

```
360   BCC error                    / length = or Q
370   STA substring_length         / save characters free
380   LDA #&FF                      / set error flag
390   STA error_flag
400   .calc_length
410   LDA string_length            / get main string's length
420   CMP offset                    / is offset within string?
430   BCS no_problems               / yes, no problems
440   LDX string_length            / else place substring
450   INX                           / at end of main string
460   STX offset
470   LDA #&FF                      / and flag that error has
480   STA error_flag                / occurred
490   CLC                           / clear carry
500   LDA string_length            / get length of string
510   ADC substring_length         / find string + substring length
520   STA string_length            / save result
530   JMP insert_substring         / move on
540   .no_problems
550   SEC                           / set carry
560   LDA string_length            / get string length
570   SBC offset                    / subtract offset
580   TAX                           / move into X for index
590   INX                           / increment index
600   LDA string_length            / get main string's length
610   STA source                    / save it
620   CLC                           / clear carry
630   ADC substring_length         / find total length
640   STA string_length            / save result
650   STA destination               / and for index
660   .make_space                   / move right of string right
670   LDY source                    / get source index
680   LDA main_string,Y            / get byte from string
```

```
690    LDY destination          / get destination index
700    STA main_string,Y        / move byte along
710    DEC destination          / decrement both indexes
720    DEC source
730    DEX                      / decrement counter
740    BNE make_space           / continue to gap made
750    .insert_substring        / get ready to move substring
760    LDA #0                   / clear accumulator
770    STA source               / and source
780    LDX substring_length     / get counter
790    .transfer
800    LDY source               / get index
810    LDA sub_string,Y         / get byte from substring
820    LDY offset               / get offset into string
830    STA main_string,Y        / and place byte in string
840    INC offset               / increment both indexes
850    INC source
860    DEX                      / decrement counter
870    BNE transfer             / continue until substring
                                  inserted
880    LDA error_flag           / get error flag
890    BNE error                / set carry if error
900    .good
910    CLC
920    BCC finish
930    .error
940    SEC
950    .finish
960    RTS
970    ] NEXT pass
980    INPUT"MAIN STRING "main_string$
990    main%=LEN(main_string$)
1000   INPUT"STRING FOR INSERTION "substring$
1010   sub%=LEN(substring$)
```

```
1020   ?string_length=main%
1030   $&3000=main_string$
1040   ?substring_length=sub%
1050   $&3100=substring$
1060   INPUT"START OF INSERTION "index%
1070   ?offset=index%
1080   CALL add_string
1090   PRINT$&3000
```

The program begins by checking the length bytes to ensure that no null strings are present (lines 150 to 220) and then sums their two lengths to obtain the final length. If the addition results in the Carry flag being set (line 270) the total length will exceed 256 bytes and as a result the substring will be truncated to the correct number of characters (lines 310 to 390).

If the insertion index is greater than the length of the string, the substring is actually concatenated on to the end of the main string. This evaluation is performed by lines 400 to 530. Before inserting the substring, all characters to the left of the index must be shuffled up through memory to make space for the substring. These calculations are carried out (lines 550 to 650) ready for the shuffling process (lines 660 to 740). Inserting the substring now simply involves copying it from its buffer into the space opened up for it (lines 750 to 870), the X register being used as the characters-moved counter.

Finally, the error flag is restored and the Carry flag conditioned to signal any errors.

5 A Bubble of Sorts

Any program written to handle quantities of data will at some time require the data in the data table to be sorted into an ordered list in ascending or descending value. Several algorithims are available to facilitate this manipulation of data, of which the bubble sort is perhaps the simplest to implement in BASIC or machine code.

The technique involves moving through the data list and comparing pairs of bytes. If the first byte is smaller than the next byte in the list, the next pair of bytes is sought. If, on the other hand, the second byte is smaller than the first, the two bytes are swapped. This procedure is repeated until a pass is executed in which no elements are exchanged and therefore all are in ascending order. Program 9 is the BASIC version of such a bubble sort.

Program 9

```
 10   REM ** BASIC BUBBLE SORT **
 20   DIM table 20
 30   FOR loop=0 TO 19
 40   READ byte
 50   table?loop=byte
 60   NEXT loop
 70
 80   REM ** Bubble up routine **
 90   FOR bubble_up=0 TO 19
100      temp=bubble_up
110
120      REPEAT
```

130   IF table?temp>table?(temp−1) THEN UNTIL TRUE :
       GOTO 190

140   hold=table?temp

150   table?temp=table?(temp−1)

160   table?(temp−1)=hold

170   temp=temp−1

180   UNTIL temp=0

190 NEXT

200

210 DATA 1,255,67,89,120

220 DATA 6,200,88,45,199

230 DATA 0,123,77,98,231

240 DATA 9,234,99,98,100

250

260 REM ** print final array **

270 FOR read=0 TO 19

280   PRINT table?read

290 NEXT read

300 END

The data bytes for sorting are held within the four data lines 210 to 240 and these are read into the vector array called table. The sorting procedure is performed by lines 120 to 180, line 130 checking to see if a swap is required.

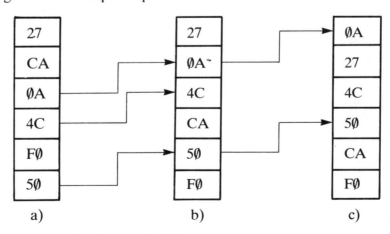

Figure 5.1   Numbers bubbling up

Figure 5.1 illustrates graphically how small numbers bubble up through a data list using this sorting method. In this example the data list consists of six numbers: 27, CA, 0A, 4C, F0 and 50 (Figure 5.1a). After the first pass of the bubble sort three swaps have occurred (Figure 5.1b) thus:

1. 27 < CA therefore no change.
2. CA > 0A therefore swap items.
3. CA > 4C therefore swap items.
4. CA < F0 therefore no change.
5. F0 > 50 therefore swap items.

The next pass through the data list produces the ordered list of Figure 5.1c in which just two swaps occurred:

1. 27 > 0A therefore swap items.
2. 27 < 4C therefore no change.
3. 4C < 50 therefore no change.
4. CA > 50 therefore swap items.
5. CA < F0 therefore no change.

All the data elements are now in their final order, so the next pass through the list will have no effect. We can signal this by using an exchange flag to indicate whether the last pass produced any swaps, exiting the sort routine when the flag is cleared. This detail is included in the assembler listed below as Program 10:

Program 10

```
10   REM ** BUBBLE SORT **
20   array_address=&70
30   address_next_byte=&72
40   length_of_array=&74
50   swap_flag=&75
60   FOR pass=0 TO 3 STEP 3
70     P%=&C00
80     [OPT pass
90     .bubble_sort
100    DEC length_of_array
110    .bubble_up_loop
120    LDY #0                    / initialize Y
```

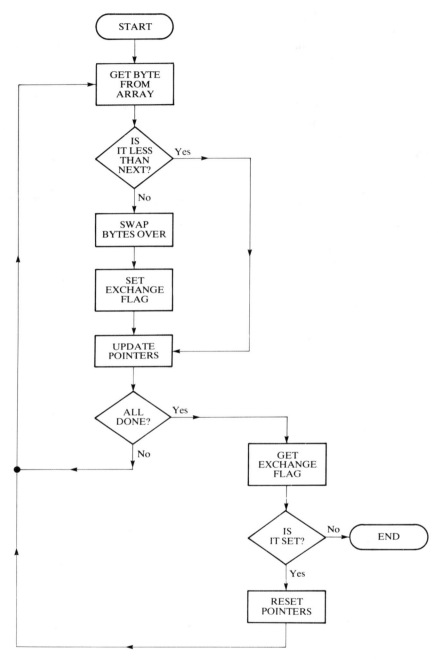

Figure 5.2   Bubble sort flowchart

```
130     STY swap_flag              / clear the swap flag
140     LDX length_of_array        / get length pointer
150     .loop
160     LDA (address_next_byte),Y  / get byte from array
170     CMP (array_address),Y      / is second byte >= first?
180     BCS second>first           / yes, so branch
190     PHA                        / no, save byte
200     LDA (array_address),Y      / get preceding byte
210     STA (address_next_byte),Y  / save in next location
220     PLA                        / restore first byte
230     STA (array_address),Y      / and complete swap
240     LDA #1                     / load accumulator with 1
250     STA swap_flag              / to indicate swap
260     .second>first
270     INY                        / move to next byte
280     DEX                        / decrement counter
290     BNE loop                   / continue to complete
300     LDA swap_flag              / get flag
310     BEQ finish                 / if clear, end
320     DEC length_of_array        / decrement outer counter
330     BNE bubble_up_loop         / repeat iteration until Z = 1
340     .finish
350     RTS
360   ] NEXT pass
370   !array_address=&4000
380   !address_next_byte=&4001
390   BYTE%=0
400   REPEAT
410      INPUT"Number"num
420      byte%?&4000=num
430      byte%=byte%+1
440      UNTIL num=-1
450   ?length_of_array=byte%-1
```

```
460   CALL &C00
470   FOR sort=0 TO byte%−1
480      PRINT sort?&4000
490   NEXT
500   END
```

The program first requests you (in BASIC!) to input a series of random integer values less than 256, which are then poked into memory. A count is kept of the number of items presented, which may be up to 256, and completes on the entry of −1. The machine code begins by decrementing the length_of_array by one (line 100). This is because the last element in the array will have no element beyond it to swap with. The swap flag is then cleared (line 130) and the main loop entered using the X register to count the iterations.

The loop begins by loading the data byte into the accumulator (line 160) and comparing it with the one immediately preceding it. If the byte+1 is greater than the byte, the Carry flag will be set and no swap required, in which case the branch to second>first is executed (line 180). If a swap is required, the second byte is saved by pushing it on to the hardware stack. The first byte is transferred to the position of the second byte (lines 200 and 210) and the accumulator restored from the stack, which is then transferred to the first byte position (lines 220 to 230). To denote that a swap has occured a 1 is placed into the swap flag byte (lines 240 and 250).

The index and counters are then adjusted (lines 270 and 280) and the loop repeated until all array elements have been compared. Upon completion of the full pass through the array the swap flag is checked. If it is clear, no exchanges took place during the last pass and so the data list is now ordered and the sort finished (lines 300 and 310). If the flag is set, the length_of_array byte is decremented and the procedure repeated once more (lines 320 and 330).

6 ASCII to Binary Conversion

An important aspect of interactive machine code is the ability to convert strings of ASCII characters into their hexadecimal equivalents so that they may be manipulated by the processor. In this chapter we examine, with program examples, how this is performed. The routines provide the following conversions:

1. Single ASCII characters into binary (hex).
2. Four ASCII hex digits into two hex bytes.
3. Signed ASCII decimal string into two signed hex bytes.

ASCII HEX TO BINARY CONVERSION

This routine will convert a hexadecimal ASCII character in the accumulator into its four-bit binary equivalent. For example, if the accumulator contains &37—that is, ASC"7"—the routine will result in the accumulator holding 7, or 00000111 binary. Similarly, if the accumulator holds &46 or ASC"F", the routine will return &F or 00001111 in the accumulator.

Conversion is, in fact, quite simple and Table 6.1 gives some indication of what is required:

Table 6.1

Hex	Binary value	ASCII value	ASCII binary
0	00000000	&30	00110000
1	00000001	&31	00110001
2	00000010	&32	00110010
3	00000011	&33	00110011
4	00000100	&34	00110100
5	00000101	&35	00110101
6	00000110	&36	00110110
7	00000111	&37	00110111

51

Table 6.1   (Contd.)

8	00001000	&38	00111000
9	00001001	&39	00111001
A	00001010	&41	01000001
B	00001011	&42	01000010
C	00001100	&43	01000011
D	00001101	&44	01000100
E	00001110	&45	01000101
F	00001111	&46	01000110

The conversion of ASCII characters 0 to 9 is straightforward. All we need to do is to mask off the high nibble of the character's ASCII code. Therefore ASC"1" is &31 or 00110001—masking the high nibble with AND &0F results in 00000001. Converting ASCII characters A to F is a little less obvious, however. If the high nibble of the code is masked off, the remaining bits are 9 less than the hex required. The ASCII for the letter 'D' is &44 or 01000100. Masking the high nibble with AND &0F gives 4, or 00000100. Adding 9 to this gives:

```
  00000100
+ 00001001
  00001101
```

the binary value for &D.

Program 11

```
 10   REM ** CONVERT ASCII CHARACTER IN **
 20   REM ** ACCUMULATOR TO BINARY **
 30   REM ** REQUIRES 20   BYTES OF MEMORY **
 40   FOR pass=0 TO 3 STEP 3
 50     P%=&C00
 60     [OPT pass
 70     .ascii_binary
 80     CMP #48                 / ASCII home cursor code
 90     BCC illegal             / control code
100     CMP #58                 / is it 0 to 9?
110     BCC zero_nine           / yes, skip A to F translation
120     SBC #7                  / jump to A to F codes
```

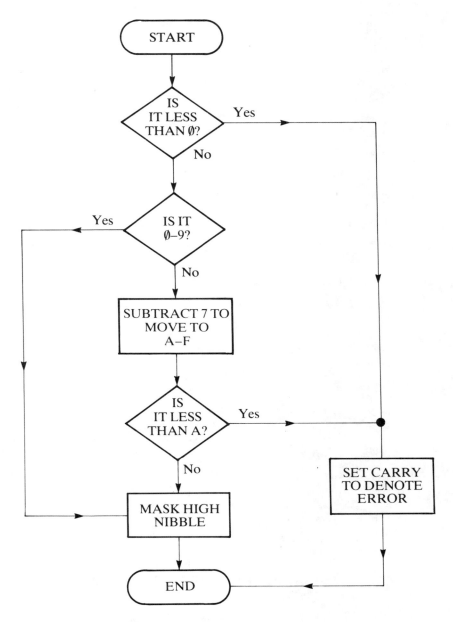

Figure 6.1   Conversion flowchart

```
130     BCC illegal          / carry set if legal
140     CMP #64              / is it higher than ' @ '?
150     BCS return           / no, illegal so return
160     .zero_nine
170     AND #&0F             / preserve low nibble
180     .return
190     RTS
200     .illegal
210     SEC                  / flag error
220     RTS
230     ] NEXT pass
240
250   REM ** TESTING ROUTINE **
260   FOR pass=0 TO 3 STEP 3
270       P%=&C80
280       [OPT pass
290       .test
300       JSR &FFE0          / osrdch
310       JSR ascii_binary
320       BCC over           / no errors
330       LDA #&FF           / carry set—error
340       .over
350       STA &70
360       RTS
370       ] NEXT pass
380   CLS
390   PRINT"HIT A HEX CHARACTER KEY, AND ITS
      BINARY"
400   PRINT"EQUIVALENT VALUE WILL BE PRINTED"
410   CALL test
420   PRINT ?&70
```

Program 11 contains a short demonstration, prompting for a hexa-decimal value key to be pressed and returning its hexadecimal code. Thus, pressing the 'A' key will produce a result of 41.

The ascii_binary routine begins by checking for the legality of the character by comparing it with 48 (&30). If the value in the accumulator is less than ASC"0" the Carry flag will be cleared, signalling an error. Assuming the character checks out okay, the contents are then compared with 58 (&3A), which is one greater than the ASCII code for 9. What this part of the routine is trying to do is to ascertain whether the accumulator's contents are in the range &30 to &39. If they are, the Carry flag will be cleared and the branch to zero_nine (lines 110 and 160) performed. The high nibble is then masked off and the conversion completed.

If the branch of line 110 fails, a legality check for the hex characters A to F is performed. This is done by subtracting 7 from the accumulator's contents, which should bring the value it holds down below 64 (&40), or one less than the ASCII code for the letter 'A'. At this point the Carry flag should be set (it was previously set as the branch of the previous line was not performed) and the CMP #64 of line 140 will clear it if the contents are higher than 64. The routine then masks off the high nibble, leaving the correct binary.

The following example shows how the conversion of ASC"F" to &F works:

Mnemonic	Accumulator	Carry flag
	&46 (ASC"F")	
CMP #&30	&46	1
BCC illegal		
CMP #&3A	&46	1
BCC zero_nine		
SBC #7	&3F	1
BCC illegal		
CMP #&40	&3F	0
BCS return		
AND &0F	&0F	0
RTS		

Note that this routine indicates an error by returning with the Carry flag set, so any calls to it should always check the Carry flag on return. The short test routine does this, and loads the accumulator with &FF to signal the fact.

Using two calls to this routine allows two-byte hex values to be input and converted into a full eight-byte value. On completion of the first call the accumulator's contents need to be shifted into the high nibble. The coding might look like this:

```
JSR osrdch              / get first character
JSR ascii_binary        / convert to binary
BCS report_error        / non-hex if C = 1
ASL A                   / move into higher nibble
ASL A
ASL A
ASL A
STA high_nibble         / save result
JSR osrdch              / get second character
JSR ascii_binary        / convert to binary
BCS report_error        / non-hex if C = 1
ORA high_nibble         / add high nibble
                        all binary now in accumulator
```

Using this routine and entering, say, &FE will return 11111110 in the accumulator.

FOUR ASCII DIGITS TO HEX

We can use the ascii_binary routine as the main subroutine in a piece of coding that will convert four ASCII digits into a two-byte hexadecimal number, making the routine useful for inputting addresses. For example, the routine would convert the ASCII string "CAFE" into a two-byte binary number 11001010 11111110 or &CAFE. Program 12 lists the entire assembler:

Program 12

```
10   REM ** CONVERT FOUR ASCII DIGITS INTO **
20   REM ** A TWO-BYTE HEXADECIMAL NUMBER **
30   buffer=&80
40   address=&70
50   osrdch=&FFE0
60   osasci=&FFE3
```

```
 70    FOR pass=0 TO 3 STEP 3
 80      P%=&C00
 90      [OPT pass
100      .address_binary
110      LDY #0                    / initialize Y
120      LDX #address              / get byte destination
130      STY 0,X                   / clear three bytes
140      STY 1,X
150      STY 2,X
160      .next_chr
170      LDA buffer,Y              / get character from buffer
180      JSR ascii_binary          / convert it to binary
190      BCS error                 / non-ASCII if carry set
200      ASL A : ASL A             / move low nibble into
210      ASL A : ASL A             / the upper nibble
220      STY 2,X                   / save buffer index
230      LDY #4                    / moving four bits
240      .again
250      ASL A                     / move bit 7 into Carry flag
260      ROL 0,X                   / move C into B0 and B7 into C
270      ROL 1,X                   / move C into B0 and B7 into C
280      DEY                       / next bit
290      BNE again                 / again, until all bits shifted
300      LDY 2,X                   / restore index
310      INY                       / and repeat
320      BNE next_chr              / loop once more
330      .error
340      LDA 2,X                   / accumulator points to illegal
                                     character
350      RTS
360      .ascii_binary
370      CMP #48
380      BCC illegal
390      CMP #58
```

```
400      BCC zero_nine
410      SBC #7
420      BCC illegal
430      CMP #64
440      BCS return
450      .zero_nine
460      AND #&ØF
470      .return
480      RTS
490      .illegal
500      SEC
510      RTS
520      ] NEXT pass
530   FOR pass=Ø TO 3 STEP 3
540      P%=&C5Ø
550      [OPT pass
560      .test
570      LDY #Ø            / set buffer index
580      LDX #4            / four characters
590      .over
600      JSR osrdch        / read keyboard
610      STA buffer,Y      / save key in buffer
620      JSR osasci        / print key pressed
630      CMP#13            / was it RETURN?
640      BEQ end           / branch if yes
650      INY               / increment index
660      DEX               / decrement character count
670      BNE over          / branch if < 5 characters
680      .end
690      JSR address_binary
700      RTS
710      ]
720      NEXT
```

730   PRINT

740   PRINT"Input a hex address without the '&' "

750   CALL test

760   PRINT

770   PRINT"First byte was :&";~?&71

780   PRINT"Second byte was :&";~?&70

The machine code begins by clearing three bytes of zero page RAM pointed to by the contents of the X register (lines 110 to 150). The ASCII characters are accessed one by one from a buffer resident anywhere in memory (line 170), though in this case it is the four bytes from &80. Conversion and error-detection are performed (lines 180 and 190) and the four returned bits shifted into the high four bits of the accumulator. The buffer index, which keeps track of the character position in the buffer, is saved in the third of the three bytes cleared.

The loop between lines 240 and 320 is responsible for moving the four bits through the two zero page bytes which house the final result. In fact, with the accumulator, the whole process of the loop is to perform the operation of a 24-bit shift register! Figure 6.2 illustrates the procedure.

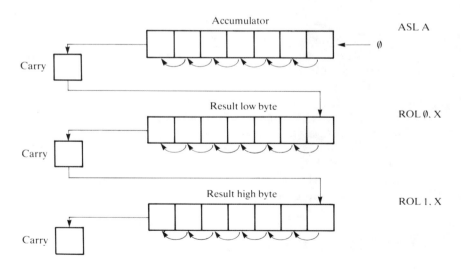

Figure 6.2   Movement of bits through a 3-byte shift register

The ASL A instruction shuffles the bits in the accumulator one bit to the left, with the dislodged bit 7 moving across into the Carry flag bit. This Carry bit is then rotated into bit Ø of the result address low byte, which in turn rotates its bit 7 into the Carry flag. The next ROL instruction repeats this movement on the high byte. The net effect of all this is that as the process is executed four times, the returned conversions are shifted through the result address to reside in the correct place as Figure 6.3 illustrates.

	1, X	Ø, X	Accumulator
Entry	00000000	00000000	11110000
1st pass	00000000	00001111	00000000
2nd pass	00000000	11110000	00000000
3rd pass	00001111	00000000	00000000
4th pass	11110000	00000000	00000000

Figure 6.3   *A 24-bit shift register, showing passage of the bits in the number &FØØØ*

Error-checking is provided for, the routine aborting when it encounters an illegal hex character, leaving the accumulator containing the index into the buffer thereby pointing to the illicit value. In fact, this method is used somewhat craftily to complete the execution of the conversion-rotate loop using a RETURN character placed at the end of the ASCII hex string.

The test routine (lines 56Ø to 69Ø) prompts for four hex based characters to be input. These are placed in the buffer (line 61Ø) and printed to the VDU. On completion of input the address_binary routine is polled, the result being placed in the first two bytes of the user area for printing or manipulation purposes.

CONVERT DECIMAL ASCII STRING TO BINARY

This routine takes a signed decimal string of ASCII characters and transforms them into a two-byte hexadecimal number. For example, entering −32,678 will return the value &8ØØØ, where &8ØØØ is its signed binary equivalent. Entry requirements to the

conversion routine are obtained by the BASIC text in lines 860 to
930. Note that in addition to obtaining the characters for insertion
into the string buffer, the number of characters for conversion is
also required, this being placed in the first byte of the buffer.

Program 13

```
10   REM ** DECIMAL ASCII TO BINARY **
20   string_index=&70
30   current=&71
40   sign_flag=&73
50   buffer=&74
60   FOR pass=0 TO 3 STEP 3
70     P%=&C00
80     [OPT pass
90     .decimal_string_hex
100    LDX buffer              / get index
110    BEQ error               / error, null string
120    LDY #0                  / clear Y register
130    STY sign_flag           / clear Sign flag
140    STY current             / clear stores
150    STY current+1
160    INY                     / increment Y
170    STY string_index        / set index past length
180    LDA buffer,Y            / get first character
190    CMP #ASC"-"             / is it a minus sign?
200    BNE positive            / no, check for positive
210    LDA #&FF                / yes, set Sign flag
220    STA sign_flag
230    INC string_index        / move on to next character
240    DEX                     / decrement length counter
250    BEQ error               / oops! error already if equal
260    JMP convert_character   / now convert digits
270    .positive
280    CMP #ASC"+"             / is it a positive sign?
```

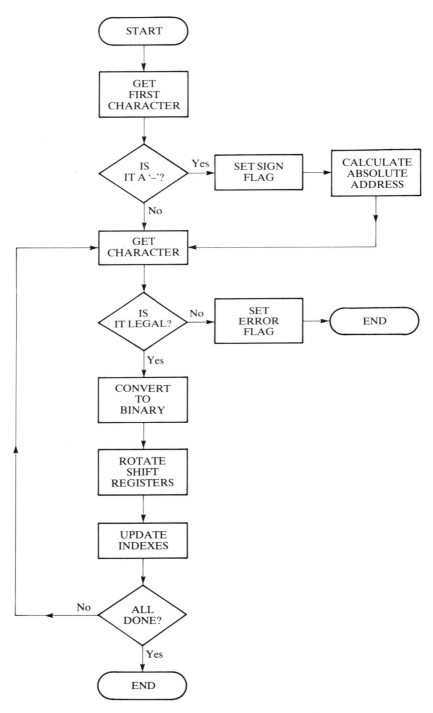

Figure 6.4   ASCII string to binary conversion flowchart

```
290    BNE check_legality        / no, make sure legal
                                    character
300    INC string_index          / yes, move to next character
310    DEX                       / decrement length counter
320    BEQ error                 / error if length now zero
330    .convert_character
340    LDY string_index          / restore index
350    LDA buffer,Y              / get character from buffer
360    .check_legality
370    CMP #ASC"9"+1             / is it <= ASCII code for 9?
380    BPL error                 / no, it's bigger—error!
390    CMP #ASC"Ø"               / is it >= ASCII code for Ø?
400    BMI error                 / no, error
410    PHA                       / save code on stack
420    ASL current               / multiply two bytes by two
430    ROL current+1
440    LDA current               / save low byte
450    LDY current+1             / save high byte
460    ASL current               / multiply by two again
                                    (now *4)
470    ROL current+1
480    ASL current               / and once again (now *8)
490    ROL current+1
500    CLC                       / clear carry
510    ADC current               / add low byte *2
520    STA current               / and save
530    TYA                       / transfer high byte *2
540    ADC current+1             / and add to *8
550    STA current+1             / current and current +1=*1Ø
560    SEC                       / set carry
570    PLA                       / restore ASCII code
580    SBC #ASC"Ø"               / convert ASCII to binary
590    CLC                       / clear carry
600    ADC current               / add it
```

```
610     STA current               / store result
620     BCC no_carry              / branch if no carry
630     INC current+1             / otherwise increment
640     .no_carry
650     INC string_index          / move index on
660     DEX                       / decrement length
670     BNE convert_character     / and do next character if not
                                    finished
680     LDA sign_flag             / get Sign flag
690     BPL no_error              / branch if positive
700     SEC                       / set carry
710     LDA #0
720     SBC current               / subtract low byte
730     STA current               / save result
740     LDA #0
750     SBC current+1             / subtract high byte
760     STA current+1             / save signed value
770     .no_error
780     CLC                       / clear carry
790     BCC finish                / and finish
800     .error
810     SEC                       / signal error
820     .finish
830     RTS
840     ]
850     NEXT pass
860   PRINT"ENTER NUMBER FOR CONVERSION ";
870   INPUT A$
880   length%=LEN(A$)
890   ?buffer=length%
900   FOR loop=1 TO length%+1
910     ascii=ASC(MID$(A$,loop,1))
920     buffer?loop=ascii
930   NEXT
```

940   CALL decimal_string_hex

950   @ %=0

960   PRINT"HEX VALUE IS : &";

970   PRINT~(!current AND &FFFF)

The machine code begins by obtaining the character count in the X register. An error is signalled if this count is zero, otherwise the program progresses, clearing the Sign flag (used to signal positive or negative values) and result destination bytes at 'current' (lines 120 to 150). Location &70 is used to hold the string_index, pointing to the next character for conversion. This byte is initially loaded with 1 so that it skips over the count byte in the buffer.

The first byte of the string is tested for a '+' or '−' sign, the former being an optional item in the string, and the Sign flag is set accordingly (lines 180 to 230). The 'convert_character' loop starts by testing the character about to be manipulated to ensure it is a decimal value, i.e. 0 to 9 inclusive. Converting the byte into binary form is facilitated by multiplying the byte by 10. This multiplication is readily available using four arithmetic shifts and an addition, giving 2*2*2+2 = 10.

Because we are dealing with a two-byte result, the arithmetic shift must be performed on the two bytes, allowing bits to be transferred from one byte to the other. This is performed by using an ASL followed by a ROL. As Figure 6.5 illustrates, this acts exactly like a 16-bit ASL. The first pass through this character conversion loop has little effect, as it is operating on characters already converted, of which there are none first time round!

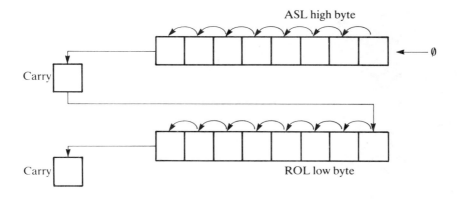

Figure 6.5   A 16-bit arithmetic shift

Lines 560 to 620 carry out and store the conversion of ASCII to binary. This is performed, as we know from earlier examples, by masking off the high nibble. Another technique for doing this is simply to subtract the ASCII code for 0, &30.

Once all the characters have been processed, the Sign flag is checked for a negative value. If this is indicated (lines 680 and 690), the value of current is subtracted from zero, thereby converting the absolute value into a signed negative byte (lines 700 to 760). The Carry flag is used to indicate any error conditions, being set to indicate that an error has occurred, and the string_index at &70 points to the illegal character.

7   Binary to Hex ASCII

This chapter complements the preceding one and illustrates how memory-based hex values can be converted into their ASCII representation. The routines provide the following conversions:

1. Print accumulator as two ASCII hex characters.
2. Print two hex bytes as four ASCII hex characters.
3. Print two-byte signed binary number as signed decimal number.

PRINT ACCUMULATOR

To convert an eight-bit binary number into its ASCII hex equivalent characters, the procedure described in Chapter 6 must be reversed. However, because text is printed on the screen from left to right, we must deal with the high nibble of the byte first. Program 14 uses the hexprint routine to print the hexadecimal value of any key pressed at the keyboard.

Program 14

```
10   REM ** PRINT ACC AS HEX NUMBER **
20   oswrch=&FFEE
30   FOR pass=0 TO 3 STEP 3
40      P%=&C00
50      [OPT pass
60      .hexprint
70      PHA                    / save accumulator
80      LSR A : LSR A          / move upper nibble
```

```
 90     LSR A : LSR A           / into lower nibble
100     JSR first               / convert first digit
110     PLA                     / restore accumulator
120     .first
130     AND #&0F                / clear high nibble
140     CMP #10                 / is it < 10?
150     BCC over                / yes, jump over
160     ADC #6                  / no, add 7, value is A–F
170     .over
180     ADC #48                 / convert to ASCII
190     JMP oswrch              / and print it
200     ] NEXT pass
210   CLS
220   PRINT"Press any key "
230   PRINT"Its hex value will be displayed"
240   BYTE%=USR(&FFE0)
250   A%=BYTE% AND &FF
260   CALL hexprint
```

The hexprint routine is embedded between lines 70 and 190. The accumulator's contents are first pushed on to the hardware stack. This is a necessary procedure as it will have to be restored before the second pass, which calculates the code for the second character. The first pass through the routine sets about moving the upper nibble of the accumulator byte into the lower nibble (lines 80 and 90). The 'first' subroutine ensures that the high nibble is cleared by logically ANDing it with &0F. This is, of course, surplus to requirement on the first pass but is needed on the second pass to isolate the low nibble.

Comparing the accumulator's contents with 10 will ascertain whether the value is in the ranges 0 to 9 or A to F. If the Carry flag is clear, it is in the lower range and simply setting bits 4 and 5, by adding &30, will give the required ASCII code. A further 7 must be added to skip non-hex ASCII codes to arrive at the ASCII codes for A to F (&41 to &46). You may have noticed that line 160 does not add 7 but in fact adds one less, 6. This is because, for this section of coding to be executed, the carry must have been set, and the 6502 addition opcode references the Carry flag for addition. Therefore the addition performed is accumulator + 6 + 1.

The JMP of line 190 will return the program back to line 110. Remember 'first' was called with a JSR so the RTS from completion of the oswrch call returns control here. The accumulator is restored and the process repeated for the second ASCII digit.

The following example works through the program's operation, assuming the accumulator holds the value 01001111, &4F:

Mnemonic	Accumulator	Carry flag
	&4F	
LSR A	&27	1
LSR A	&13	1
LSR A	&09	1
LSR A	&04	1
JSR first		
AND #&0F	&04	1
CMP #10	&04	0
BCC over		
.over		
ADC #&30	&34 (ASC"4")	0
JMP oswrch		
PLA	&4F	0
AND #&0F	&0F	0
CMP #10	&0F	1
BCC over		
ADC #6	&16	0
.over		
ADC #&30	&46 (ASC"F")	0
JMP oswrch		

PRINT A HEXADECIMAL ADDRESS

The hexprint routine can be extended to enable two zero page bytes to be printed out in hexadecimal form. This is an especially important procedure when writing machine based utilities, such as a hex dump or disassembler. The revamped program is listed below:

Program 15

```
10   REM ** PRINT TWO HEX BYTES AS **
20   REM ** A TWO BYTE ADDRESS **
30   address=&70
```

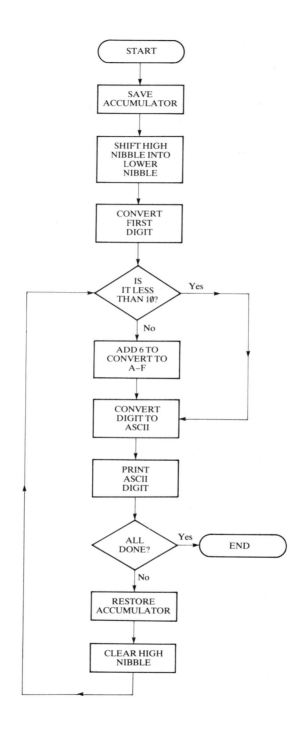

Figure 7.1   Hex to ASCII conversion flowchart

```
40    oswrch=&FFEE
50    FOR pass=0 TO 3 STEP 3
60       P%=&C00
70       [OPT pass
80       .address_print
90       LDX #address          / X register points to address
100      LDA 1,X               / get high byte of address
110      JSR hexprint          / and print it
120      LDA 0,X               / get low byte of address
130      JSR hexprint          / and print it
140      RTS
150      .hexprint
160      PHA                   / save accumulator
170      LSR A : LSR A         / move upper nibble
180      LSR A : LSR A         / into lower nibble
190      JSR first             / convert first digit
200      PLA                   / restore accumulator
210      .first
220      AND #&0F              / clear high nibble
230      CMP #10               / is it <10?
240      BCC over              / yes, jump over
250      ADC #6                / no, add 7, value is A−F
260      .over
270      ADC #48               / convert to ASCII
280      JMP oswrch            / and print it
290      ]
300      NEXT pass
310   END
```

Zero paged indexed addressing is used to access the two bytes, the crucial location being given in the X register, which acts as the index for the high byte, LDA 1,X (line 100), and the low byte, LDA 0,X (line 120). The all-important address in this instance is &70 (line 30), so the bytes accessed by 'address_print' are &70 (&70+0) and &71 (&70+1). Using this method, various addresses can be housed within zero page and any of them reached simply by seeding the X register with the locational value.

BINARY SIGNED NUMBER TO SIGNED ASCII DECIMAL STRING

This conversion utility takes a two-byte hexadecimal number and converts it into its equivalent decimal-based ASCII character string. For example, if the two-byte value is &7FFF the decimal string is 32,767, &7FFF being 32,767 in decimal. The coding uses signed binary values so that if the most significant bit is set, a negative value is interpreted. This is relayed in the string with a minus sign. This means that the routine can handle values in the range 32,767 to −32,768. When using the routine, remember that the two's complement representation is used, so that a hex value of &FFFF is converted to the string −1, and &8000 returns the character string '−32,767'.

The two address bytes are located in the zero page bytes &70 and &71 and the string buffer from &75 onwards. The length of the string buffer will vary, but its maximum length will not exceed six digits, therefore this number of bytes should be reserved.

Program 16

```
 10   REM ** BINARY SIGNED NUMBER CONVERSION **
 20   REM ** INTO SIGNED DECIMAL ASCII STRING **
 30   binary_address=&70
 40   temporary=&72
 50   sign_flag=&74
 60   buffer=&75
 70   FOR pass=0 TO 3 STEP 3
 80     P%=&C00
 90     [OPT pass
100     .hex_decimal_string
110     LDY #0              / clear Y register
120     TYA                 / and accumulator
130     STA buffer          / and then the buffer
140     STA buffer+1
150     STA buffer+2
```

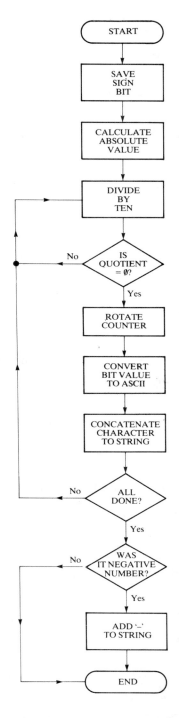

Figure 7.2   Binary to ASCII string conversion flowchart

```
160    STA buffer+3
170    STA buffer+4
175    STA buffer+5
180    LDA binary_address+1    / get high byte and use to
190    STA sign_flag           / set or clear negative flag
200    BPL conversion          / branch if positive, i.e. > &80
210    SEC                     / set carry
220    TYA                     / clear accumulator
230    SBC binary_address      / subtract to get absolute
                                  binary_address
240    STA binary_address      / and save
250    TYA                     / clear accumulator
260    SBC binary_address+1    / repeat with high byte
270    STA binary_address+1    / and save again
280    .conversion
290    LDA #0                  / clear accumulator
300    STA temporary           / and temporary store
310    STA temporary+1
320    CLC
330    LDX #16                 / sixteen bits to do
340    .loop
350    ROL binary_address      / move bit 7 into carry
360    ROL binary_address+1    / and on into bit 0
370    ROL temporary           / move bit 7 into carry
380    ROL temporary+1         / and on into bit 0
390    SEC                     / set carry
400    LDA temporary           / get low byte of temp
410    SBC #10                 / subtract ten
420    TAY                     / save result in Y
430    LDA temporary+1         / get high byte temp
                                  binary_address
440    SBC #0                  / subtract carry bit
450    BCC less_than           / branch if divisor W dividend
460    STY temporary           / else save result of operation
```

470	STA temporary+1	/ i.e. dividend–divisor
480	.less_than	
490	DEX	/ decrement bit count
500	BNE loop	/ branch until 16 bits done
510	ROL binary_address	/ rotate bit 7 into carry
520	ROL binary_address+1	/ and on into bit 0
530	.add_ascii	
540	CLC	/ clear carry
550	LDA temporary	/ get low byte temp
560	ADC #ASC"0"	/ convert to ASCII character code
570	JSR concatenate	/ add it to string in buffer
580	LDA binary_address	/ get low byte binary address
590	ORA binary_address+1	/ or with high byte. Result = 0 if all done
600	BNE conversion	/ not finished, repeat
610	.finished	
620	LDA sign_flag	/ get sign
630	BPL positive	/ no sign if positive
640	LDA #ASC"–"	/ include minus sign if > &7FFF
650	JSR concatenate	/ add it to front of string
660	.positive	
670	RTS	/ subroutine to form ASCII character string in buffer
680		
690	.concatenate	
700	PHA	/ save accumulator
710	LDY#0	
720	LDA buffer,Y	/ get buffer length
730	TAY	/ and use as index
740	BEQ zero_finish	/ finished if zero length
750	.shuffle_along	
760	LDA buffer,Y	/ get character from buffer
770	INY	/ increment index

```
780     STA buffer,Y          / and shuffle characters along
790     DEY : DEY             / restore original
                                  binary_address minus 1
800     BNE shuffle_along     / continue until all shuffled up
                                  one place
810     .zero_finish
820     PLA                   / restore accumulator
830     LDY#1                 / point beyond length byte
840     STA buffer,Y          / place character in buffer
850     DEY
860     LDX buffer,Y          / get string length
870     INX
880     STX buffer,Y          / save length
890     RTS                   / string printing routine
900
910     .string_print
920     LDX buffer
930     LDY #1
940     .print_loop
950     LDA buffer,Y
960     JSR &FFE3
970     INY : DEX
980     BNE print_loop
990     RTS
1000    ]NEXT pass
1010    PRINT"INPUT HEX VALUE FOR CONVERSION";
1020    INPUT" : &" hex$
1030    hex$="&"+hex$
1040    hex%=EVAL(hex$)
1050    !binary_address=hex%
1060    CALL hex_decimal_string
1070    CALL string_print
```

To demonstrate the routine's workings, the program first prompts for a hexadecimal number. This is evaluated and placed at 'binary_ address'.

The program proper starts by clearing the string buffer area (lines 110 to 175), an important procedure that ensures no illicit characters find their way into the ASCII string. The sign of the number is tested by loading the high byte of the address byte into the accumulator and saving its value in the sign_flag byte. This process will condition the Negative flag. If it is set, a negative number is detected and the plus branch to conversion (line 200) fails. The next seven operations obtain the absolute value of the two-byte number by subtracting it from itself and the set carry bit. Thus &FFFF will result in an absolute value of 1 and &8000 an absolute value of 32,678.

The two flows rejoin at line 280, where the two temporary bytes are cleared. These bytes are used in conjunction with the 'binary_ address' bytes to form a 32-bit shift register, allowing bits to flow from the low byte address to the high byte of temporary.

The loop of lines 340 to 520 performs the conversion by successively dividing through by ten until the quotient has a value of zero. By this time the binary equivalent of the ASCII character being processed will reside in the temporary byte. To produce this, the loop needs 16 iterations and the X register is used to count these out. Converting the binary to hex simply involves adding &30 or ASC"0" to it (lines 530 to 560).

It may not be immediately clear what is happening. Table 7.1 shows the values of the accumulator and four associated bytes after each of the 16 passes of the loop when converting &FFFF into its absolute ASCII value of 1. It should be clear from this how the bits shuffle their way through the four-byte 'register'.

Table 7.1

Iteration	Accumulator	&70	&71	&72	&73
1	00	01	00	00	00
2	FF	02	00	00	00
3	FF	04	00	00	00
4	FF	08	00	00	00
5	FF	10	00	00	00
6	FF	20	00	00	00
7	FF	40	00	00	00
8	FF	80	00	00	00
9	FF	00	00	01	00
10	FF	00	00	01	00
11	FF	00	00	01	00

Table 7.1 (Contd.)

12	FF	00	00	01	00
13	FF	00	00	01	00
14	FF	00	00	01	00
15	FF	00	00	01	00
16	FF	00	00	01	00

All that is now required is for this character to be added to the string buffer. This concatenation is completed in the assembler of lines 690 to 890. This began by obtaining the buffer index, which contains the current number of characters already concatenated. This is actually stored in the first byte of the buffer, &75 in this instance. It is then moved across into the accumulator. Next, lines 750 to 800 move any characters present in the buffer up memory one byte, thereby opening up a gap of one byte into which the newly formed character can be placed (lines 820 to 890). The buffer index is also incremented and restored at this point before an RTS is made back to the main body of the program.

End of program operation is tested for by logically ORing the contents of the high and low bytes of the address. If the result is zero all bits have been rotated and dealt with, in which case the sign_flag byte is tested to ascertain whether a minus sign need be placed at the start of the ASCII string (lines 620 to 670).

8 Printing Print!

Every machine code program sooner or later requires text to be printed on to the screen. In most instances this involves simply indexing into an ASCII string table and printing the characters, using one of the Operating System calls, until either a RETURN character or zero byte is encountered. Program 17 uses this, the simplest of methods.

Program 17

```
 10   REM ** PRINT STRING FROM MEMORY **
 20   string%=&4000
 25   osasci=&FFE3
 30   FOR pass=0 TO 3 STEP 3
 40     P%=&C00
 50     [OPT pass
 60     .string_print
 70     LDX #0                  / initialize index
 90     .next_character
100     LDA string%,X           / get character
110     JSR osasci              / print it
120     INX                     / increment index
130     CMP #13                 / was it RETURN?
140     BNE next_character      / no, repeat
150     RTS
160     ] NEXT pass
170   CLS
```

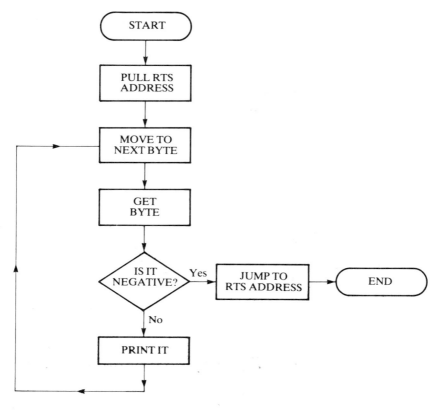

Figure 8.1   Printing embedded code flowchart

    18Ø   INPUT"String to be printed :"$&4ØØØ
    19Ø   CALL string_print

Here, a string buffer is located at &4ØØØ and the requirement for printing the string is that it must be terminated with a ASCII RETURN, &ØD. The program begins by initializing an index, the X register (line 8Ø), and loading the byte at buffer+X into the accumulator. This is printed using OSASCI, the index is incremented and then the accumulator's contents are compared to see if the character just output was a RETURN (line 13Ø). If not, the loop branches back and the next character is sought.

As you are probably aware, BBC BASIC includes two OS calls that allow text to be output to the screen: OSASCI and OSWRCH. They operate in slightly different ways. Which one you use depends on the kind of screen formatting you anticipate. The difference in their operation is in the way they action the RETURN character (13 or &ØD). If OSASCI encounters this it moves the cursor to the start of the current line and then down one line. OSWRCH operates only on the first step and does not move the cursor down. To generate the line-feed using OSWRCH the accumulator must be loaded first with 10 and then 13 and the OS calls performed:

```
LDA #10
JSR OSWRCH
LDA #13
JSR OSWRCH
```

Alternatively, a JSR OSNEWL could replace these two calls with the same effect.

Program 18 depicts how several strings may be printed to the screen using a loop similar to that described above. The number of strings for printing may be variable, the desired number being passed into the routine via the Y register. The string data has been entered using the EQUS command (BASIC I owners can use the $ operator as described in Chapter 2) to form a look-up table at the top of the machine code. Control characters have been embedded into the textual strings so that double-height, flashing and coloured text can be produced.

If a large amount of string data is to be stored, and the amount to be printed at any one time varied, a vectored address accessing the table should be used. Positioning of the text on the screen can be performed by using the operating system TAB function provided by OSWRCH. The accumulator should contain 9 and the index registers the tab co-ordinates.

Program 18

```
 10   REM ** PRINT STRING **
 20   string%=&4000
 30   osasci=&FFE3
 40   FOR pass=0 TO 3 STEP 3
 50     P%=&C00
 60     [OPT pass
 70     .string_print
 80     LDX #0                    / set index start
 90     LDY #4                    / no. of string to print
100     .next_character
110     LDA string%,X             / get character
```

```
120     JSR osasci              / print it
130     INX                     / increment index
140     CMP #13                 / is it a RETURN?
150     BNE next_character      / no, continue
160     DEY                     / yes, count string number
170     BNE next_character      / continue until all printed
180     RTS
190     ] NEXT pass
200     P% = &4000
210     [.table_of_strings
220     EQUW &8D0C
230     EQUS" BBC MICRO"
240     EQUW &8D0D
250     EQUS" BBC MICRO"
260     EQUW &880D
270     EQUS" FLASHING TEXT"
280     EQUW &830D
290     EQUS" AND COLOURED TEXT"
300     EQUB 13
310     ]
320     CALL string_print
```

The final program in this chapter shows the way I find easiest to store and print character strings, stowing them directly into the machine code. The two main advantages of this method are that the string is inserted directly at the point it is needed, thus avoiding the need to calculate indexes into look-up tables, and that it is fully relocatible, because it manipulates it own address.

Program 19

```
10      REM ** PRINT ASCII STRING STORED **
20      REM ** WITHIN BODY OF MACHINE CODE**
30      low_byte=&70 : high_byte=&71
40      osasci=&FFE3
50      FOR pass=0 TO 3 STEP 3
```

```
 60    P%=&C00
 70    [OPT pass
 80    .ascii_print
 90    PLA                    / get low byte return address
100    STA low_byte           / and save it
110    PLA                    / get high byte return address
120    STA high_byte          / and save it
130    .main_loop
140    LDY #0                 / initialize index
150    INC low_byte           / increment low_byte
160    BNE continue           / branch if not zero
170    INC high_byte          / increment page
180    .continue
190    LDA (low_byte),Y       / get ASCII character
200    BMI end_of_string      / branch if byte negative
210    JSR osasci             / print character
220    JMP main_loop          / repeat once more
230    .end_of_string
240    JMP (low_byte)         / back to machine code!
250    ]NEXT pass
260
270  REM *** EXAMPLE OF USE ***
280  P%=&C50
285  [.example
290                           / first the machine code
300    LDA #12                / ASCII clear screen
310    JSR osasci             / print it!
320    JSR ascii_print        / call printing routine
330                           / now leave assembler and insert
                                 string
340  ]
350  $P%="Strings within Machine Code!"
360  P%=P%+LEN($P%)
370  [
```

```
380   NOP                    / negative byte &EA = 11101010
390   LDA #7                 / bell character
400   JSR osasci
410   RTS
420   ]
430   CALL example
```

The ASCII character string is placed in memory by leaving the assembler (line 340) and using the Program Counter, P%, as the string's argument. The string is defined (line 350) and P% reset beyond the string's length (line 360). BASIC II owners need not leave the assembler in this instance, simply replacing lines 340, 350, 360, and 370 with the single line:

```
340   EQUS "Strings within Machine Code!"
```

For this routine to work, it is imperative that the first byte following the string is a negative byte—that is, one with bit 7 set. The opcode for NOP, &EA, is ideal for this purpose.

The ascii_print routine is just 27 bytes in length and it should be called as a subroutine immediately before the string is encountered. On entry into the subroutine, the first four operations pull the return address from the stack and save it in a zero page vector, low_byte and high_byte. These bytes are then incremented by one to point at the byte following the subroutine call.

Because the string data follows on immediately after the 'ascii_print' subroutine call (see Table 8.1), post indexed indirect addressing can be used to load the first string character into the accumulator (line 190). The string terminating negative byte is tested for (line 200) and if not found the byte is printed with an OSASCI call. A JMP main_loop is then performed and the loop repeated once more. When the negative byte is encountered, and the branch of line 200 succeeds, an indirect jump (line 240) via the current vectored address is executed, returning control back to the calling machine code at the end of the ASCII string.

Using this method, control codes may also be placed within the string so that they may be printed to the desired effect for coloured text, double-height text and so forth.

Table 8.1 String storage 'within' program

Address	Hex	Mnemonic/character
&C5Ø	A9	LDA #
&C51	ØC	12
&C52	2Ø	JSR
&C53	E3	FFE3
&C54	FF	
&C55	2Ø	JSR
&C56	ØØ	CØØ
&C57	ØC	
&C58	53	S
&C59	74	t
&C5A	72	r
&C5B	69	i
&C5C	6E	n
&C5D	67	g
&C5E	73	s
&C5F	2Ø	
&C6Ø	77	w
&C61	69	i
&C62	74	t
&C63	68	h
&C64	69	i
&C65	6E	n
&C66	2Ø	
&C67	4D	M
&C68	61	a
&C69	63	c

Table 8.1   (Contd.)

&C6A	68	h
&C6B	69	i
&C6C	6E	n
&C6D	65	e
&C6E	2Ø	
&C6F	43	C
&C7Ø	6F	o
&C71	64	d
&C72	65	e
&C73	21	!
&C74	EA	NOP
&C75	A9	LDA #
&C76	Ø7	7
&C77	4C	JMP
&C78	E3	FFE3
&C79	FF	

9 Hexvar

The Hexvar utility is especially useful when it comes to debugging BASIC programs. It would be an ideal routine to add to the wedge described earlier and is a most powerful tool when used in conjunction with *CLEAR (see Chapter 2).

When run, Hexvar provides a listing of the values held in the integer variables A% to Z%, as illustrated in Figure 9.1. The format produced by the routine is not unlike that produced by the word indirection operator. In conjunction with *CLEAR it becomes an invaluable debugging aid. Initializing all variables to zero before running a BASIC program and then producing a dump of their values at various points in the program will give a good indication as to where the trouble lies in a malfunctioning program. The temporary halts can be induced by moving an END statement through the program.

```
A%=&00000041
B%=&281A1A19
C%=&35AC9E56
D%=&53332A18
E%=&1B38148F
F%=&8CD7F292
G%=&B942D2DD
H%=&718CBE76
I%=&00000000
J%=&2A100EA5
K%=&000000FF
L%=&EF11E1F7
M%=&69978662
N%=&00000000
O%=&00002500
P%=&00000C58
```

Figure 9.1   Hexvar output

```
Q%=&9962C0CF
R%=&60BD966C
S%=&69380DA5
T%=&00000100
U%=&0000007B
V%=&00000000
W%=&9B053F20
X%=&00000000
Y%=&0000000A
Z%=&709AF8A2
```

Figure 9.1   (Contd.)

Variable	Associated bytes			
A%	404	405	406	407
B%	408	409	40A	40B
C%	40C	40D	40E	40F
D%	410	411	412	413
E%	414	415	416	417
F%	418	419	41A	41B
G%	41C	41D	41E	41F
H%	420	421	422	423
I%	424	425	426	427
J%	428	429	42A	42B
K%	42C	42D	42E	42F
L%	430	431	432	433
M%	434	435	436	437
N%	438	439	43A	43B
O%	43C	43D	43E	43F
P%	440	441	442	443
Q%	444	445	446	447
R%	448	449	44A	44B
S%	44C	44D	44E	44F
T%	450	451	452	453
U%	454	455	456	457
V%	458	459	45A	45B
W%	45C	45D	45E	45F
X%	460	461	462	463
Y%	464	465	466	467
Z%	468	469	46A	46B

Figure 9.2   Integer variable byte allocation

Each of the Beeb's 26 integer variables is allocated four bytes of memory in block zero RAM from &404 to &468 inclusive. Figure 9.2 shows the bytes allocated to each variable. The variable @% is allocated four bytes from &400, and although this is an integer variable, it is not included in the listing because it is normally reserved for PRINT formatting purposes. It could be included, if required, by modifying lines 290 and 390 of the following program.

Program 20

```
 30    REM ** PRINT HEXADECIMAL VALUES OF ALL **
 40    REM ** INTEGER VARIABLES, A% TO Z% **
 50    oswrch=&FFEE
 60    osasci=&FFE3
 70    FOR pass=0 TO 3 STEP 3
 80      P%=&C00
 90      [OPT pass
100      .variable_dump
110      LDA #14              / paged mode on
120      JSR oswrch
130      LDX #4               / 4 bytes per variable
140      LDA #ASC"A"          / first variable is A
150      PHA                  / save ASCII code on stack
160      .next_variable       / main loop
170      PLA                  / get variables code
180      JSR oswrch           / print it
190      TAY:INY              / transfer and increment code
200      TYA:PHA              / restore and push
210      LDA #ASC"%"          / print '%' sign
220      JSR oswrch
230      LDA #ASC"="          / print '=' sign
240      JSR oswrch
250      LDA #ASC"&"          / print hex sign
260      JSR oswrch
270      LDY#4                / Y counts 4 bytes
280      .next_byte
```

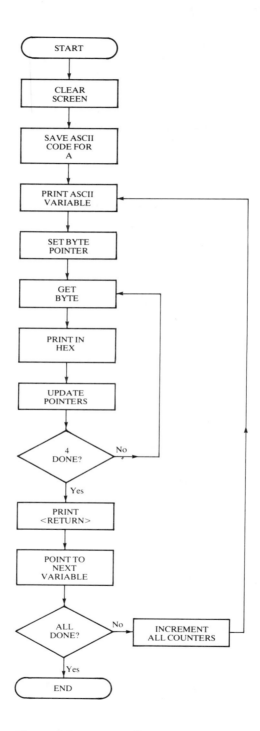

Figure 9.3   Hexvar flowchart

```
290    LDA &403,X              / get byte

300    JSR hexprint            / print it in hex

310    DEX : DEY               / move on to next byte

320    BNE next_byte           / continue for 4 bytes

330    LDA#13                  / print carriage return

340    JSR osasci

350    CLC                     / clear Carry flag

360    TXA                     / move index into accumulator

370    ADC #8                  / add 8 to get least significant
                                 byte of next variable

380    TAX                     / restore index

390    CPX #108                / last variable (Z%) done?

400    BNE next_variable       / no, repeat again

410    PLA                     / finished. Get surplus byte
                                 from stack

420    LDA #15                 / paged mode form feed

430    JSR oswrch

440    RTS

450

460    .hexprint

470    PHA                     / save accumulator

480    LSR A : LSR A           / move upper nibble

490    LSR A : LSR A           / into lower nibble

500    JSR first               / convert first digit

510    PLA                     / restore accumulator

520    .first

530    AND #&0F                / clear high nibble

540    CMP #10                 / is it < 10?

550    BCC over                / yes, jump over

560    ADC #6                  / no add 7, value is A−F

570    .over

580    ADC #48                 / convert to ASCII

590    JMP oswrch              / and print it

600    ]
```

610   NEXT pass

620   END

The program itself uses indexed addressing (lines 160 to 400) to read each of a variable's four bytes in turn into the accumulator, and the Hexprint subroutine described in Chapter 7 to output each byte to the screen in hexadecimal ASCII form. Figure 9.3 charts the program flow. The ASCII code for each of the variables is saved in a single byte—initially &41, which is ASC"A"—which is pushed and pulled on to the hardware stack, being incremented each time through the .next_variable loop (lines 140, 150 and 190, 200).

Because the output is slightly longer than can be output to the MODE 7 screen without scrolling, the routine begins by putting the Beeb in Paged mode, by printing an ASCII 14 code (line 110 and 120). This is reversed on program exit (lines 420 and 430).

The program could be extended to print variable values in signed decimal form using the 'hex to signed decimal conversion' routine described in Chapter 7.

10 Move, Fill and Dump

MOVE IT!

The ability to move blocks of memory around within the bounds of the memory map is a necessity. An example application for this routine is in relocating programs loaded from disc into RAM from &19∅∅ down to the tape default value of PAGE at &E∅∅ so that they can be run correctly. Alternatively, the program could be used to relocate sections of machine code rather than rewriting the assembler that created them, assuming your code has been designed to make it portable.

At first sight it may seem that the simplest method of moving a block of memory is to take the first byte to be moved and store it at the destination address, take the second byte and place it at the destination address+1, and so forth. There would be no problem here if the destination address were outside the source address, but consider what would happen if the destination address was within the bounds to be searched by the source address and the two regions overlapped.

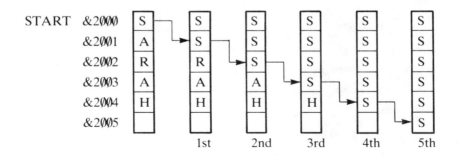

Figure 10.1   The overwriting move sequence

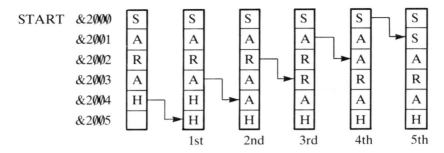

START &2000
&2001
&2002
&2003
&2004
&2005

1st   2nd   3rd   4th   5th

Figure 10.2   The correct move sequence

Figure 10.1 illustrates the problem using this straightforward method to move a block of five bytes forward by just one byte, in other words to relocate five bytes from, say, &2000 to &2001. The first character 'S' is stored at location &2001, thereby overwriting the 'A'. The program then takes the next character—the one at START+1—which was the 'S' just moved, and copies it to START+2 or &2002. You can see the end result for yourself. The whole block is filled with 'S's—not the required effect.

To avoid this, the MOVE routine acts intelligently and if it finds that an overwrite would occur, executes the movement of bytes in reverse order starting at the highest address and moving down the memory map, as in Figure 10.2.

Program 21

```
10   REM ** MEMORY BLOCK MOVE ROUTINE **
20   REM ** 109 bytes long when assembled **
30   REM ** plus 5 data bytes in zero page **
40   length=&70 : REM low byte
50   length_high_byte=&71
60   destination=&72 : REM low byte
70   destination_high_byte=&73
80   source=&74 : REM low byte
90   source_high_byte=&75
100  FOR pass=0 TO 3 STEP 3
110    P%=&C00
```

```
120    [OPT pass
130    .memmove
140    SEC                            / set carry
150    LDA destination                / get low byte
160    SBC source                     / subtract low byte source
170    TAX                            / transfer result
180    LDA destination_high_byte      / get high byte
190    SBC source_high_byte           / subtract source high byte
200    TAY                            / transfer result
210    TXA                            / restore low byte result
220    CMP length                     / compare low byte length
230    TYA                            / restore high byte result
240    SBC length_high_byte           / compare high byte length
250    BCS move_left                  / if carry set move left
260    BCC move_right                 / else move right
270    .move_left
280    LDY #0                         / clear index
290    LDX length_high_byte           / get whole page index
300    BEQ left_partial_page          / if zero do part page
310    .left_complete_pages
320    LDA (source),Y                 / get source byte
330    STA (destination),Y            / copy to destination
340    INY                            / increment index
350    BNE left_complete_pages        / do until all done
360    INC source_high_byte           / increment page counters
370    INC destination_high_byte
380    DEX                            / decrement loop count
390    BNE left_complete_pages        / redo loop until loop
                                        exhausted
400    .left_partial_page
410    LDX length                     / get part page length
420    BEQ exit                       / finish if zero
430    .last_left
440    LDA (source),Y                 / get source byte
```

```
450    STA (destination),Y          / copy byte to destination
460    INY                          / increment index
470    DEX                          / decrement count
480    BNE last_left                / repeat until done
490    .exit
500    RTS                          / finished!

510                                 / *********************
520    .move_right
530    CLC                          / clear carry
540    LDA length_high_byte         / get length high byte
550    PHA                          / save on stack
560    ADC source_high_byte         / add to source high byte
570    STA source_high_byte         / save result
580    CLC                          / reclear carry
590    PLA                          / get length of high byte
600    ADC destination_high_byte    / add to destination high
                                       byte
610    STA destination_high_byte    / save result
620    LDY length                   / get low byte length
630    BEQ right_complete_pages     / branch if zero
640    .transfer
650    DEY                          / decrement index
660    LDA (source),Y               / get source byte
670    STA (destination),Y          / copy to destination
680    CPY #0                       / is Y = 0?
690    BNE transfer                 / no, repeat
700    .right_complete_pages
710    LDX length_high_byte         / get number of pages
720    BEQ exit                     / if zero finish
730    .update
740    DEC source_high_byte         / decrement page high bytes
750    DEC destination_high_byte
760    .page
```

```
770    DEY                        / decrement index
780    LDA (source),Y             / get source byte
790    STA (destination),Y        / copy to destination
800    CPY#0                      / branch if Y = 0
810    BNE page
820    DEX                        / decrement count
830    BNE update                 / repeat until done
840    RTS
850    ]NEXT
860    INPUT"START ADDRESS : &"START$
870    START$="&"+START$
880    START%=EVAL(START$)
890    INPUT"DESTINATION : &"DEST$
900    DEST$="&"+DEST$
910    DEST%=EVAL(DEST$)
920    INPUT"LENGTH : &"LGTH$
930    LGTH$="&"+LGTH$
940    LGTH%=EVAL(LGTH$)
950    !length=LGTH%
960    !destination=DEST%
970    !source=START%
980    CALL memmove
```

When run, the BASIC text requests for three inputs: the start
address of the memory block, its destination address and its length.
All values should be entered as hex values. Thus to move a 1K
block of memory from &2000 to &4000, the values to input are:

START ADDRESS	&2000
DESTINATION	&4000
LENGTH	&400

where &400 = 1024 in decimal. Note that as with most of the
programs in this book only the digits of the address need be
entered. Omit the '&'.

For reasons explained, the coding begins by ascertaining
whether a left-move or right-move operation is required. It calcu-

lates this (lines 14Ø to 21Ø) by subtracting the source address from the destination address. If the result is less than the number of bytes to be moved then an overlap will occur and the left_move coding is called. If there is no overlap the quicker right_move coding is executed.

For further descriptive purposes we'll examine the left_move routine (lines 27Ø to 5ØØ). Memory movement is done in two phases. First, complete memory pages, as given by the high_byte_ length, are relocated, followed by any remaining bytes as indicated in length.

To start, the number of pages to be moved is loaded into the X register (line 29Ø), and a branch to left_partial_page made if it is zero (line 3ØØ). Transfer of data bytes is completed using post-indexed indirect addressing through the zero page vectors (lines 31Ø to 39Ø). When all pages have been moved any remaining bytes are transferred by the left_partial_page loop (lines 4ØØ to 48Ø).

The right-move routine is similar in operation except that it starts at the highest memory location and moves down the memory map, the highest address of source and destination being first calculated by lines 53Ø to 83Ø.

FILL

Program 22 gives the assembler listing to implement a memory fill routine, useful for clearing sections of RAM with a predefined value.

Program 22

```
10   REM ** MEMORY FILL ROUTINE **
20   REM ** 30 bytes long when assembled **
30   REM ** plus 5 data bytes in zero page **
40   fill_data=&70
50   length_low_byte=&71
60   length_high_byte=&72
70   start_address_high_byte=&74
80   start_address_low_byte=&73
90   FOR pass=0 TO 3 STEP 3
100     P%=&C00
110     [OPT pass
```

```
120     .memfill
130     LDA fill_data                           / get data to poke
140     LDX length_high_byte                    / get number of bytes
                                                    to fill
150     BEQ partial_page                        / if zero just do rest of
                                                    page
160     LDY #0                                  / clear Y
170     .complete_page
180                                             / fill all complete
                                                    memory pages
190     STA (start_address_low_byte),Y          / fill byte
200     INY                                     / increment index
210     BNE complete_page                       / repeat until page
                                                    done
220     INC start_address_high_byte             / increment page
230     DEX                                     / decrement page
                                                    counter
240     BNE complete_page                       / continue until page
                                                    done
250     .partial_page
260                                             / fill partial page
                                                    remaining
270     LDX length_low_byte                     / get bytes left to fill
280     BEQ finish                              / if none then finish
290     LDY #0                                  / clear index
300     .again
310     STA (start_address_low_byte),Y          / fill byte
320     INY                                     / increment index
330     DEX                                     / decrement byte
                                                    counter
340     BNE again                               / do until page done
350     .finish
360     RTS
370     ]
380     NEXT pass
390   INPUT"INPUT FILL VALUE : &"fill$
```

```
400   fill$="&"+fill$
410   fill%=EVAL(fill$)
420   INPUT"INPUT START ADDRESS : &"start$
430   address$="&"+start$
440   address=EVAL(address$)
450   INPUT"INPUT LENGTH : &"length$
460   length$="&"+length$
470   length=EVAL(length$)
480   ?fill_data=fill%
490   !length_low_byte=length
500   !start_address_low_byte=address
510   CALL memfill
```

The coding expects to find the fill value, start address and amount of memory to be filled in five zero page bytes from &70. Input of these is handled by a few lines of BASIC. To clear a 1K block of memory from &3000 with zero, the following information should be typed in response to the prompts:

INPUT FILL VALUE	&00
INPUT START ADDRESS	&3000
INPUT LENGTH	&E00

The filling procedure is executed in lines 130 to 350 using a whole page and partial page movement technique as described earlier.

A MEMORY DUMP

A hex and ASCII dump of memory can be of great use, not only within machine code programs, but also when used from a BASIC program. Most often it provides information about the way a program is manipulating numeric and string variables and tables. Figure 10.3 shows the type of dump produced by the routine: 24 lines of eight bytes each. The example shows part of the BASIC interpreter, in fact the BASIC look-up table. Each line starts with the current address, followed by the eight bytes stored in memory from that point. The far right of the listing provides the ASCII equivalents of each byte. Any non-ASCII character (one greater than &7F) or control code (less than &20) is represented by a full stop.

```
8070    8A 41 4E 44 80 00 41 42    .AND..AB
8078    53 94 00 41 43 53 95 00    S..ACS..
8080    41 44 56 41 4C 96 00 41    ADVAL..A
8088    53 43 97 00 41 53 4E 98    SC..ASN.
8090    00 41 54 4E 99 00 41 55    .ATN..AU
8098    54 4F C6 10 42 47 45 54    TO..BGET
80A0    9A 01 42 50 55 54 D5 03    ..BPUT..
80A8    43 4F 4C 4F 55 52 FB 02    COLOUR..
80B0    43 41 4C 4C D6 02 43 48    CALL..CH
80B8    41 49 4E D7 02 43 48 52    AIN..CHR
80C0    24 BD 00 43 4C 45 41 52    *..CLEAR
80C8    D8 01 43 4C 4F 53 45 D9    ..CLOSE.
80D0    03 43 4C 47 DA 01 43 4C    .CLG..CL
80D8    53 DB 01 43 4F 53 9B 00    S..COS..
80E0    43 4F 55 4E 54 9C 01 44    COUNT..D
80E8    41 54 41 DC 20 44 45 47    ATA. DEG
80F0    9D 00 44 45 46 DD 00 44    ..DEF..D
80F8    45 4C 45 54 45 C7 10 44    ELETE..D
8100    49 56 81 00 44 49 4D DE    IV..DIM.
8108    02 44 52 41 57 DF 02 45    .DRAW..E
8110    4E 44 50 52 4F 43 E1 01    NDPROC..
8118    45 4E 44 E0 01 45 4E 56    END..ENV
8120    45 4C 4F 50 45 E2 02 45    ELOPE..E
8128    4C 53 45 8B 14 45 56 41    LSE..EVA
```

Figure 10.3   Output produced by the memory dump

As it stands, the routine requires three zero page data bytes, two for the start address and one for the number of eight byte lines to be dumped. The routine also employs the address_print and hexprint routines discussed earlier.

Program 23

```
10   REM ** DUMP LINES OF 8 BYTES OF **
20   REM ** MEMORY IN HEX AND ASCII **
30   address=&70
40   lines=&73
```

```
 5Ø    oswrch=&FFEE
 6Ø    FOR pass=Ø TO 3 STEP 3
 7Ø      P%=&CØØ
 8Ø      [OPT pass
 9Ø      .memory_dump
1ØØ      JSR address_print        / print address
11Ø      .hex_bytes
12Ø      LDX #7                   / eight bytes to do
13Ø      LDY #Ø                   / clear index
14Ø      .hex_loop
15Ø      LDA(address),Y           / get byte
16Ø      JSR hexprint             / print it
17Ø      JSR space                / followed by a space
18Ø      INY                      / increment index
19Ø      DEX                      / decrement count
2ØØ      BPL hex_loop             / continue for 8 bytes
21Ø      JSR space                / plus a space
22Ø      .ascii_bytes
23Ø      LDX #7                   / set count
24Ø      LDY #Ø                   / clear index
25Ø      .ascii_loop
26Ø      LDA(address),Y           / get byte
27Ø      CMP #&2Ø                 / is it a control code?
28Ø      BMI full_stop            / yes, print full stop
29Ø      CMP #&8Ø                 / is it a graphics code?
3ØØ      BCC leap_frog            / no, leap over
31Ø      .full_stop
32Ø      LDA #ASC"."              / illegal, get code for "."
33Ø      .leap_frog
34Ø      JSR oswrch               / print contents of accumulator
35Ø      INY                      / increment index
36Ø      DEX                      / decrement count
37Ø      BPL ascii_loop           / continue until done
```

```
380    LDA#13               / print a RETURN
390    JSR &FFE3
400    CLC                  / clear carry
410    LDA address          / get low byte of address
420    ADC #8               / add 8 to it
430    STA address          / save result
440    BCC no_carry         / branch if no carry over
450    INC address+1        / otherwise increment page
460    .no_carry
470    DEC lines            / decrement lines printed count
480    BNE memory_dump      / repeat if not done
490    RTS                  / back to BASIC
500    .space
510    LDA #32              / print a space
520    JMP oswrch
530    .address_print
540    LDX #address         / X register points to the
550    LDA 1,X              / two byte address
560    JSR hexprint         / stored in zero page
570    LDA 0,X
580    JSR hexprint
590    JSR space
600    JSR space
610    RTS
620    .hexprint
630    PHA                  / save accumulator
640    LSR A : LSR A        / move upper nibble
650    LSR A : LSR A        / into lower nibble
660    JSR first            / convert first digit
670    PLA                  / restore accumulator
680    .first
690    AND #&0F             / clear high nibble
700    CMP #10              / is it < 10?
```

```
710    BCC over              / yes, jump over
720    ADC #6                / no add 7, value is A−F
730    .over
740    ADC #48               / convert to ASCII
750    JMP oswrch            / and print it
760    ] NEXT
770    INPUT"Dump address :&"hex$
780    hex$="&"+hex$
790    hex%=EVAL(hex$)
800    !address=hex%
810    ?lines=24
820    CALL memory_dump
```

Program operation is quite simple, using the X register to count the bytes as they are printed across the screen using hexprint (lines 120 to 210). The second section of code (lines 220 to 370) is responsible for printing either the ASCII character contained in the byte or a full stop if a non-printable or control code is encountered. The final section of code moves the cursor down one line and increments the address counter. The whole loop is repeated until the line count reaches zero.

11 Monitoring Machine Code

The following program shows how several of the routines discussed earlier can be utilized to produce a simple machine code monitor type program which allows the user to move either forwards or backwards through the memory map and alter the contents of any location as desired.

Program 24

```
10   REM ** A SIMPLE MACHINE CODE MONITOR **
20   REM ** USES RETURN, DELETE, & A FOR ALTER **
30   address=&70
40   high=&73
50   low=&74
60   osasci=&FFE3
70   FOR pass=0 TO 3 STEP 3
80     P%=&C00
90     [OPT pass
100    .display_change
110    JSR address_print      / print current address
120    LDY #0                 / clear index
130    LDA #ASC":"            / print a colon
140    JSR osasci
150    JSR space              / print a space
160    LDA (address),Y        / get byte at address
170    JSR hexprint           / print it in hex
180    JSR space              / print a space
```

```
190    .get_key              / get command key
200    JSR &FFE0
210    CMP #&1B              / was it ESCAPE?
220    BNE no_escape         / no, so branch
230    LDA #&7E              / yes, inform the MOS
240    JSR &FFF4
250    BRK                   / break to print RETURN
260    EQUB 13
270    EQUS"Finished"        / and message
280    BRK
290    .no_escape
300    CMP #127              / was it DELETE?
310    BEQ backwards         / yes, so branch
320    CMP #13               / was it a RETURN?
330    BEQ forwards          / yes, so branch
340    CMP #ASC"A"           / was it the 'A' key?
350    BEQ alter             / yes, so branch
360    BNE get_key           / no legal command so repeat
370    .alter                / alter contents of RAM
380    LDA #7                / print a BELL
390    JSR osasci
400    JSR space             / print a space
410    LDA #ASC".".          / print two full stops
420    JSR osasci
430    JSR osasci
440    LDA #8                / move cursor back to
450    JSR osasci            / first full stop
460    JSR osasci
470    JSR check_digit       / get and check first digit
480    JSR ascii_binary      / convert to binary
490    ASL A : ASL A         / shift into high nibble
500    ASL A : ASL A
510    STA high              / save high nibble
```

520	JSR check_digit	/ get and check second digit
530	JSR ascii_binary	/ convert to binary
540	STA low	/ save result
550	ORA high	/ add two bits together
560	STA (address),Y	/ peek into memory
570	.forwards	/ move forward one byte
580	CLC	/ clear carry
590	LDA address	/ get low byte
600	ADC #1	/ add one to it
610	STA address	/ save result
620	BCC leap	/ leap over if no carry
630	INC address+1	/ else increment page
640	.leap	
650	JMP carriage_return	/ issue a RETURN
660	.backwards	/ move backwards a byte
670	SEC	/ set carry
680	LDA address	/ get low byte
690	SBC #1	/ subtract one
700	STA address	/ save result
710	BCS carriage_return	/ leap over if still set
720	DEC address+1	/ else decrement page
730	.carriage_return	
740	LDA #13	/ print a RETURN
750	JSR osasci	
760	JMP display_change	/ back to start
770		/ *** subroutines ***
780	.check_digit	
790	JSR &FFE0	/ get key from keyboard
800	CMP #ASC"G"	/ was it > 'F'?
810	BPL illegal_character	/ yes, illegal hex
820	CMP #ASC"A"	/ was it < 'A'?
830	BPL zero_nine	/ yes, check for 0-9
840	JMP osasci	/ print character A-F

```
850     .zero_nine
860     CMP #ASC"9"+1          / was it > 9?
870     BMI illegal_character  / yes, non-hex
880     CMP #ASC"0"            / was it < '0'?
890     BMI illegal_character  / yes, non-hex
900     JMP osasci            / print character 0-9
910     .illegal_character
920     LDA #7                / issue a BELL
930     JSR osasci
940     JMP check_digit       / get keyboard again
950     .address_print        / print two bytes as
960     LDX #address          / hex number
970     LDA 1,X
980     JSR hexprint
990     LDA 0,X
1000    JSR hexprint
1010    .space                / print a space
1020    LDA #32
1030    JMP osasci
1040    .hexprint
1050    PHA                   / save accumulator
1060    LSR A : LSR A         / move upper nibble
1070    LSR A : LSR A         / into lower nibble
1080    JSR first             / convert first digit
1090    PLA                   / restore accumulator
1100    .first
1110    AND #&0F              / clear high nibble
1120    CMP #10               / is it < 10?
1130    BCC over              / yes, jump over
1140    ADC #6                / no add 7, value is A-F
1150    .over
1160    ADC #48               / convert to ASCII
1170    JMP osasci            / and print it
```

```
1180    .ascii_binary
1190    CMP #ASC"A"        / is it < A?
1200    BMI nine_zero      / yes, so branch
1210    SBC #7             / subtract 7
1220    .nine_zero
1230    AND #&0F           / save low nibble
1240    RTS
1250    ] NEXT
1260    !address=&3000
```

The address from which the monitor begins displaying memory contents is obtained by the coding from the two zero page bytes &70 and &71. In this instance it has been placed there using the word indirection operator in line 1260, &3000 in this case. Using the hex address input routine described in Chapter 6 would allow the machine code to operate independently of BASIC.

The display is initialized by using the address_print subroutine to write the current hex address to the screen (line 110). This is followed by a colon (line 130 and 140) and then the hexadecimal value of the byte located at the address displayed (lines 160 to 180). Program flow is then transferred to the OSRDCH routine, which waits for one of three keys to be pressed. Note that as part of the key-checking procedure the ESCAPE key is tested for. ALL ESCAPEs must be acknowledged with an OSBYTE call. Failure to do so will result in the program 'hanging-up'. This is true for any machine code that uses the key detection routines. If an ESCAPE is detected (line 210) the OSBYTE call with the accumulator containing &7E is performed (lines 230 and 240). On return a BRK is executed and the error message 'Finished' printed.

Pressing the DELETE key causes the program to step back a single byte; pressing the RETURN key moves the program on to the next byte. Pressing the A key will allow you to enter two hexadecimal digits, which will be evaluated and then poked into the currently displayed address. Error-checking ensures that only legal hexadecimal characters are accepted.

As the monitor stands at present it is somewhat dry and, apart from allowing you to enter machine code programs in traditional form, is probably of limited use. In the rest of this commentary we shall look at ways of improving the basic module. The final version is left for you to construct to suit your needs.

Here is a list of the sort of items we could add to the monitor:

1.   Display and alter register contents.

2. Display and alter the status register in binary notation.
3. Display the stack contents.
4. Display and alter contents of the user area of zero page.
5. Run a section of machine code.

THE REGISTERS

Displaying the register's contents is quite straightforward, though a couple of points should be remembered. Firstly, any transfer of data to and from registers affects the bits in the status register flags. Secondly, to print the contents of a register requires the use of the accumulator, therefore its contents are liable to change due to overwriting.

Both pitfalls can be avoided by saving register contents on to the hardware stack before printing, thus:

```
.register_save      PHP     / save status
                    PHA     / save accumulator
                    TXA
                    PHA     / save X register
                    TYA
                    PHA     / save Y register
```

The index registers can now be printed by copying them into the accumulator once more using a transfer instruction and calling the OSWRCH routine. Remember that the transfer instructions do not affect the register they are moving from, but will overwrite the destination register. Once printed, the index registers can be restored and the accumulator and status registers printed and then themselves restored. If so required, the stack pointer could also be accessed using the TSX and TXS opcodes.

THE INS AND OUTS OF BINARY

A more useful representation of the status register's contents is in binary—we are concerned with the condition of specific bits rather than the overall value of its contents. Program 25 is a short program which produces this output, printing the binary value of a decimal number input from the keyboard. This can readily be adapted to suit your personal needs and added to the monitor.

110

Program 25

```
10   REM ** PRINT ACCUMULATOR AS A **
20   REM ** BINARY NUMBER **
30   FOR PASS=0 TO 3 STEP 3
40     P%=&C00
50     [OPT PASS
60     .binary_out
70     LDX #8              / eight bits to do
80     PHA                 / save accumulator
90     .next_bit
100    PLA                 / get accumulator
110    ASL A               / move bit 7 into carry
120    PHA                 / save shifted accumulator
130    LDA #ASC"0"         / get ASCII code for '0'
140    ADC #0              / add carry
150    JSR &FFE3           / print code for '0' or '1'
160    DEX                 / decrement bit count
170    BNE next_bit        / continue until done
180    PLA                 / balance push
190    RTS
200    ]
210    NEXT PASS
220  INPUT"A DECIMAL NUMBER :" A%
230  PRINT"BINARY EQUIVALENT:";
240  CALL binary_out
250  PRINT
```

The comments should make the machine code's operation fairly obvious.

Reversing the process would allow the status register to be loaded with a binary value, as Program 26 demonstrates:

Program 26

```
10   REM ** INPUT A HEX NUMBER IN BINARY FORM **
```

```
 20   FOR pass=0 TO 3 STEP 3
 30     P%=&2000
 40     [OPT pass
 50     .binary_in
 60     LDX #8              / eight bits to read
 70     LDA #0              / clear accumulator
 80     PHA                 / push on to stack
 90     CLC                 / clear carry
100     .loop
110     JSR &FFE0           / call osrdch
120     CMP #ASC"1"         / was it a 1?
130     BEQ SET             / yes, branch
140     CMP #ASC"0"         / was it a 0?
150     BNE LOOP            / no, redo loop
160     CLC                 / clear carry
170     BCC OVER            / and jump over
180     .SET
190     SEC                 / 1 pressed so set carry
200     .OVER
210     PHP                 / save Carry flag
220     JSR &FFE3           / print key pressed
230     PLP                 / restore carry
240     PLA                 / restore accumulator
250     ROL A               / move carry into bit 0
260     PHA                 / save accumulator
270     DEX                 / decrement bit count
280     BNE LOOP            / branch until done
290     PLA                 / pull accumulator
300     STA &70             / save result
310     RTS
320     ]NEXT pass
330   CALL binary_in
340   PRINT~?&70
```

The program scans the keyboard until it detects a pressed 1 or Ø key. Depending on which of the two is pressed, the Carry flag is set or cleared respectively. A copy of the accumulator, initially cleared, is kept on the stack and the carry bit rotated into it. This loop is executed eight times, and upon completion the accumulator holds the completed binary input.

STACKS OF MEMORY

Displaying the contents of either the stack or the user area of RAM is simple enough. Using indexed addressing, contents can be obtained from their base addresses of &1ØØ and &7Ø respectively. When displaying the stack contents remember that the stack 'grows' down memory, so the bytes between &1DØ and &1FF are probably of most use. The following mnemonics illustrate the stack method and could easily be adapted to obtain the user RAM between &7Ø and &8F:

```
.stack_print   LDY #&DØ           / start index
.stack_loop    JSR address_print  / print address X points to
               LDA &1ØØ,Y         / get byte
               JSR hexprint       / print it in hex
               INY                / increment index
               BNE stack_loop     / repeat until Y = Ø
```

MACHINE CODE FROM MACHINE CODE

When a section of code is not functioning as intended, it is often useful to run small sections of it and obtain register contents at its completion. These can then be compared with what is expected and often the bug wormed out. The easiest way to do this is to use three bytes of memory that can be called as a subroutine, but which will then jump to the section of code to be run. The return point within the code can be set with an RTS instruction entered with the monitor.

Figure 11.1 illustrates an example. Consider that we have set aside the three memory bytes from &CØØ to be our jump register. The first byte at &CØØ will always contain the opcode for JMP, which is &4C. Using the monitor, the address of the code to be executed can be seeded into the bytes at &CØ1 and &CØ2. If the run address was &2345, &C∅1 would contain the low byte and &C∅2 the high byte, so that disassembling location &C∅∅ would produce:

JMP &C∅∅   4C   ∅∅   ∅C

The coding associated when run would then execute JSR &C∅∅, which would in turn cause a jump to the specified address. Control is returned to the monitor when the previously placed RTS is encountered where register contents can be updated.

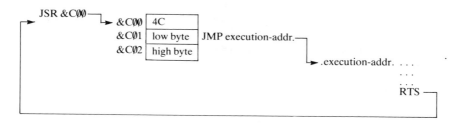

Figure 11.1   Implementing a jump register

12 Software Stack

One of the criticisms of the 6502 processor is that it has a very limited set of operation instructions—only 56, although addressing modes extend this to 152 functions. With some thought, however, it is possible to implement operations present on other processors such as the Z80 or 6809 and build up a set of useful subroutines which can ultimately be strung together to perform sophisticated operations. It will also make conversion of programs written for other processors much easier.

The routine described below mimics an instruction in the 6809 instruction set that allows the contents of up to eight registers to be 'pushed' on to a stack in memory. This stack is often known as the user stack. I say 'up to eight registers', because the ones actually pushed can be selected, this being determined by the bit pattern of the byte after the user stack subroutine call. But more of that in a moment. First, which registers are we going to push? Obviously all the processor registers: the Program Counter, Status register, accumulator and the two Index registers. The three remaining ones, we will implement as three two-byte 'pseudo-registers' from the user area of zero page. These are:

PR1 : &80 and &81

PR2 : &82 and &83

PR3 : &84 and &84

This now enables us to save the contents of these locations when required.

As already stated, the byte after the user stack subroutine call determines by its bit pattern which registers are to be pushed, as follows:

bit 0   Pseudo-register 1

bit 1   Pseudo-register 2

bit 2   Pseudo-register 3

bit 3   Y register

bit 4   X register

bit 5   Accumulator

bit 6   Status register

bit 7   Program Counter

The rule here is if the bit is set, the related register is pushed. Thus the instructions:

JSR user_stack

EQUB &FF

would push all registers on to the user stack, the embedded byte being &FF or 11111111. Alternatively, the coding:

JSR user_stack

EQUB &1E

where &1E = 00011110 would push only the accumulator, Status and Index registers. Perhaps a doubt is running through your mind: 'But the embedded byte will cause my program to crash'. Well that's true on face value, but what we do is get the user stack coding to move the program counter on one byte to pass over it. Here's the program:

Program 27

```
10   REM ** USER STACK **
20   address=&70
30   zero_page=&80
40   ?&70=12:?&71=&30
50   FOR PASS=0 TO 3 STEP 3
60     P%=&2800
70     [OPT PASS
80     .push_stack
90     PHP                    / save all processor registers
100    PHA                    / on the hardware stack
110    TXA
```

116

```
120    PHA
130    TYA
140    PHA
150    TSX                        / move stack pointer into X
160    LDY #6                     / set index
170    .push_zero_page
180    LDA zero_page−1,Y          / push zero page bytes
190    PHA                        / on to hardware stack
200    DEY                        / decrement index
210    BNE push_zero_page         / continue until done
220    INC &105,X                 / increment low byte RTS
                                     address

230    LDA &105,X                 / get it and save
240    STA zero_page              / in zero page
250    BNE pc_low                 / if not equal branch
260    INC &106,X                 / else increment page byte
270    .pc_low
280    LDA &106,X                 / get it and save
290    STA zero_page+1            / to form vector points to
                                     data byte

300    LDA #&87                   / bit code, tells register size
310    STA zero_page+2            / save it
320    LDA (zero_page),Y          / get embedded code
330    STA zero_page+3            / and save
340    LDA #8                     / eight bits to test
350    STA zero_page+4            / save it
360    DEY                        / decrement Y to &FF
370    DEC address+1              / decrement high byte
                                     address

380    .rotate_byte
390    ROL zero_page+3            / move code bit into carry
400    BCC bit_clear              / if clear skip
410    LDA &106,X                 / otherwise get byte from
                                     stack
420    STA (address),Y            / save it on user stack
```

```
430    DEY                          / decrement index
440    BIT zero_page+2              / is it a two byte register?
450    BPL bit_clear                / no, branch
460    LDA &105,X                   / yes, get second byte
470    STA (address),Y              / and save on user stack
480    DEY                          / decrement index
490    .bit_clear
500    DEX                          / decrement hardware stack
                                       offset
510    ROL zero_page+2              / move bit of register code
                                       into C
520    BCC over                     / branch if carry clear
530    DEX                          / else decrement stack offset
540    .over
550    DEC zero_page+4              / decrement counter
560    BNE rotate_byte              / do again until eight bits
                                       done
570    SEC                          / set carry
580    TYA                          / move user stack pointer
                                       into accumulator
590    ADC address                  / add low byte address
600    STA address                  / save result
610    BCC clear_stack              / skip if no carry
620    INC address+1                / else increment high byte
630    .clear_stack
640    LDX #0                       / clear X register
650    .repeat
660    PLA                          / pull byte
670    STA zero_page,X              / and restore zero page
680    INX                          / increment index
690    CPX #6                       / all bytes restored?
700    BNE repeat                   / no, branch
710    PLA                          / yes, so restore all original
720    TAY                          / register values
730    PLA
```

```
740    TAX
750    PLA
760    PLP
770    RTS                         / and back to BASIC
780    .test
790    LDA #&F0                    / seed registers
800    LDX #&F
810    LDY#&FF
820    JSR push_stack
830    EQUB &FF                    / register print code
840    RTS
850    ]NEXT
860 CLS
870 FOR N=&80 TO &85:?N=N:NEXT
880 FOR N=&3000 TO &300A:?N=0:NEXT
890 CALL test
900 FOR N=&3000 TO &300B
910    READ NAME$
920    PRINT NAME$;
930    PRINT ~?N
940    NEXT
950 DATA"ZERO PAGE ","ZERO PAGE+1",
    "ZERO PAGE+2"
960 DATA"ZERO PAGE+3","ZERO PAGE+4",
    "ZERO PAGE+5"
970 DATA "Y REGISTER ","X REGISTER "
980 DATA "ACCUMULATOR","STATUS "
990 DATA "PC LOW ","PC HIGH "
```

The question to answer next is where to place the user stack. This will depend on your own requirements, so to make the whole thing flexible, a vectored address in the bytes at &70 and &71 contains the stack address. In the program listed above, this is &3012 (line 40). The vectored address is actually the address+12. This is because the stack is pushed in reverse (decreasing) order.

When executed, the coding first pushes all the processor registers on to the hardware stack and moves the stack pointer across into the X register (lines 90 to 150). Next, the six zero page pseudo-registers are pushed there (lines 160 to 210). The return address from the subroutine call is then incremented on the stack using the contents of the X register (stack pointer) to access it (lines 220 to 270). The two bytes that form the RTS address are copied into the pseudo-register 1 (now safely on the hardware stack) to form a vector through which the embedded data byte can be loaded into the accumulator and then saved for use in zero page (lines 280 to 330).

In line 300 a pre-defined byte is loaded into the accumulator and saved in zero page. This byte holds a bit code that will inform the coding as to whether the register being pulled from the hardware stack for transfer to the software stack is one or two bytes long. The byte value, &87, is 10000111 in binary and the set bits correspond to the two-byte registers, the program counter and the three pseudo-registers. By rotating this byte left after each pull operation and using the BIT operation the Negative flag can be tested to see if a further pull is needed. All this and the copy hardware stack/push software stack is handled by the lines 340 to 560.

Finally, the registers and pseudo-registers are restored to their original values (lines 640 to 770). The test routine between lines 780 and 840 shows the way the program is used. BASIC I owners should replace the EQUB command (line 830) with the following lines:

```
830  ]
831  ?P%=&FF
832  P%=P%+1
833  [
```

The program could be extended to provide a routine to perform a pull user stack, to copy a software stack's contents into the processor and pseudo-registers.

13 Disassembling Assembler

One of the best ways of learning how to write machine code is to work through machine code routines written by 'experts'. For example, looking at the coding of the BASIC interpreter or MOS would reveal many of the Beeb's hidden secrets and would probably allow you to exploit its operation more effectively. However, working through hex dumps is extremely tedious, requiring continual cross-references to opcode charts. The obvious solution is to write a program that will take an opcode from memory, convert it into its more readily understood mnemonic format and print it, along with any required operand information—in short a disassembler.

To write a disassembler in BASIC would be the simplest solution, but we're dealing with machine code so the program supplied is an assembler version of a disassembler!

There are three main methods of writing a machine code disassembler. The simplest is to use look-up tables, employing the peeked opcode to index them and extract the relative information, but this is a bit long-winded and not very efficient. The most efficient method is to use the individual bit patterns of opcodes and rotate these for evaluation, but this is complex and not easily explained here. The third method, and the one I've chosen, is a combination of the above using a look-up table, a data table and a table of coded bytes which hold information relating to the opcode's addressing mode and byte numbers.

Program 28 lists the BASIC and assembler text for the disassembler.

The DATA tables make the whole thing look awesome, but by making effective use of the programmable function and cursor control keys, they can be entered quickly. Figure 13.1 flowcharts the disassembler's operation and if referred to in conjunction with the comments in the listing, the techniques involved in writing the program should become clearer.

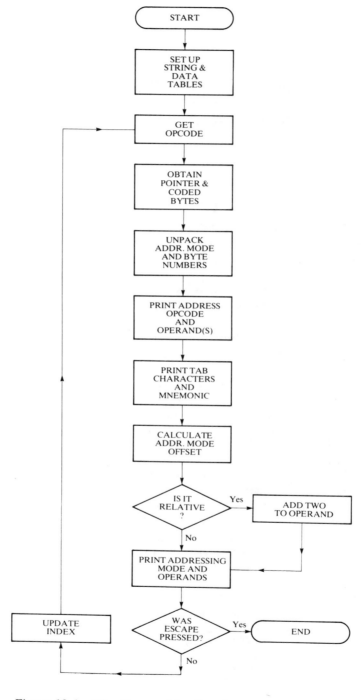

Figure 13.1   The disassembler flowchart

The coding generated by the text is the longest in this book, being a little over 1K in length as it stands, so choose the assembly area with care. The program places it in memory from &4000 (line 160), but obviously this can be altered to suit your own needs.

The mnemonic look-up table is created in lines 190 to 290. This table contains all of the 6502's 56 mnemonics in string form. Line 260 contains a pseudo-mnemonic 'ERR' and this is used by the disassembler whenever it encounters an opcode that is not used by the 6502 (these are the ones marked 'reserved for future expansion' by the designers!). The ERR is short for ERRor but you can change it if you wish. Some disassemblers use '***' or '???' instead to denote an unrecognized opcode. The remaining lines in this look-up table (lines 260 to 290) hold the addressing mode and tabulating information. The exclamation marks are used to signal to the disassembler that the operand information needs to be displayed in their place. Table 13.1 illustrates each addressing mode as it appears here.

Table 13.1

Line no.	Representation	Addressing Mode	Example
260	A	Accumulator	LSR A
260	&!!!!	Absolute	LDA &7C00
260	&!!	Zero Page	LDA &70
270	#&!!	Immediate	LDA #&FF
270	&!!!!,X	Absolute,X	LDA &7C00,X
280	&!!!!,Y	Absolute,Y	LDA &4000,Y
280	(&!!,X)	Pre-indexed	LDA (&70,X)
280	(&!!),Y	Post-indexed	LDA (&70),Y
280	&!!,X	Zero Page,X	LDA &70,X
290	&!!	Relative	BNE &03
290	(!!!!)	Indirect	JMP (&0070)
290	&!!,Y	Zero Page,Y	LDX &70,Y

CODED BYTES

The data table held between lines 320 and 570 inclusive provides the disassembler with details of each opcode as follows:

1. The number of bytes in each operation.
2. The addressing mode.

To pack this information into a single byte use the high nibble to hold the byte number and the low nibble for the addressing mode. Table 13.2 supplies the meaning of each byte code used.

Table 13.2

Code		Binary		Addressing	Example
dec	hex	hi	lo		
16	&10	0001	0000	Implied	BRK
17	&11	0001	0001	Accumulator	LSR A
35	&23	0010	0011	Zero Page	LDA &70
36	&24	0010	0100	Immediate	LDA #&FF
39	&27	0010	0111	(Zero Page,X)	LDA (&72,X)
40	&28	0010	1000	(Zero Page),Y	LDA (&74),Y
41	&29	0010	1001	Zero Page,X	LDA &00,X
42	&2A	0010	1010	Relative	BNE back
44	&2C	0010	1100	Zero Page,Y	LDX &70,Y
50	&32	0011	0010	Absolute	LDA &7C00
53	&35	0011	0101	Absolute,X	LDA &7C00,X
54	&36	0011	0110	Absolute,Y	LDX &7C00,Y
59	&38	0011	1011	(Indirect)	JMP (&0070)

The high nibble can have three values which directly reflect the operation byte numbers. These are:

0001 — 1 byte
0010 — 2 bytes
0011 — 3 bytes

The low (addressing mode) nibbles look disjointed but, as we shall see, when manipulated provide an index into the mnemonic string/ addressing mode table discussed above.

The last of the three tables (lines 620 to 980) is simply an indexing table, with each byte pointing to its mnemonic within the mnemonic look-up table. Thus the first byte, &1E (30), points to the mnemonic with opcode &00, BRK in fact. Similarly &66 points to the mnemonic for opcode &01, ORA (Zero Page,X), and so forth. At the top of this table a further three bytes are poked into memory using the word indirection operation. These bytes 1, 3 and 6 (line 1050) are used to tabulate the listing produced, keeping it neat and tidy.

THE PROGRAM

The Program Counter, P%, is reset before entering the assembler (line 1070) to ensure that the code is assembled directly above the data tables. Lines 1080 to 1210 set up the various registers with address and index details, locating the opcode to be disassembled in line 1200.

The disassembly subroutine begins by using the opcode in the Y register as an index to the mnemonic pointer table (line 620 onward), to extract the correct index into the mnemonic string table. This is saved in 'pointer' (line 1370). Using the same technique, the coded byte is extracted from the coded byte table and preserved in the X register (lines 1380 and 1390). The addr_mode nibble is masked off and the result saved. Similarly, the lower nibble is masked off and the high nibble rotated into the low nibble (lines 1430 to 1480) to give the total number of bytes within the instruction.

The next part of the program (lines 1490 to 1770) is responsible for printing the hexadecimal values of the opcode and operand(s), if any. Using the no_bytes value (line 1790), the tabulation value mentioned earlier is extracted from the index table and the appropriate number of 'spaces' printed (lines 1800 to 1870).

The mnemonic representation of the opcode is extracted from the mnemonic string table and printed (lines 1880 to 1950) using the pointer extracted earlier, and a character counter in the Y register. Next, the addressing mode format is derived by calculating an index into the mnemonic string table. This is done by rotating left the low nibble bits of the addr_mode nibble (lines 1980 to 2040) and subtracting its original value. For example, if accumulator addressing is being used the nibble value in addr_mode will be 0001. Rotating this left three times will produce 1000 (&08), and subtracting the original value will give 0111 (&07). Thus, the index from the base address given in line 2170 will be 7.

Before reaching that point, however, the byte is compared with &0A to see if relative addressing is being used. If it is, the operand low-byte value is updated to give the correct address for the branch destination (lines 2090 to 2130). Note that only the low-byte address for the branch destination is provided. The addressing mode format, which is seven bytes long in all cases (including spaces) is then printed after the mnemonic (lines 2160 to 2410). If a '!' is encountered (line 2180) the operand value(s) are output instead.

Figure 13.2 shows a typical listing produced by the machine code disassembler.

*** MACHINE CODE DISASSEMBLER ***

address	opcode	mnemonics
&E000	20 04 E0	JSR &E004
&E003	40	RTI
&E004	BD 12 DF	LDA &DF12,X
&E007	30 0E	BMI &17
&E009	98	TYA
&E00A	BC 12 DF	LDY &DF12,X
&E00D	18	CLC
&E00E	65 F2	ADC &F2
&E010	AA	TAX
&E011	98	TYA
&E012	A4 F3	LDY &F3
&E014	90 01	BCC &17
&E016	C8	INY
&E017	60	RTS
&E018	AE 4B 02	LDX &024B
&E01B	30 04	BMI &21
&E01D	38	SEC
&E01E	4C E7 DB	JMP &DBE7
&E021	A4 E6	LDY &E6
&E023	A2 04	LDX #&04

press SHIFT to continue listing

Figure 13.2   The disassembler in action

Program 28

```
10    REM *** MACHINE CODE DISASSEMBLER ***
20    CLS
30    address=&70
40    index=&72
50    no_bytes=&73
60    addr_mode=&74
70    pointer=&75
80    operand_high=&76
90    operand_low=&77
100   oswrch=&FFEE
110   osnewl=&FFE7
120   PRINT
130   PRINT"Please wait : Processing assembler"
140   PRINT
150   PRINT"Errors will be reported"
160   PRINT
170   REM *** mnemonics table ***
180   tables%=&5000
190   mne$="ADCANDASLBCCBCSBEQBITBMI"
200   mne$=mne$+"BNEBPLBRKBVCBVSCLCCLDCLI"
210   mne$=mne$+"CLVCMPCPXCPYDECDEXDEYEOR"
220   mne$=mne$+"INCINXINYJMPJSRLDALDXLDY"
230   mne$=mne$+"LSRNOPORAPHAPHPPLAPLPROL"
240   mne$=mne$+"RORRTIRTSSBCSECSEDSEISTA"
250   mne$=mne$+"STXSTYTAXTAYTSXTXATXSTYA"
260   mne$=mne$+"ERRA &!!!! &!! "
270   mne$=mne$+"#&!! &!!!!,X&!!!!,Y"
280   mne$=mne$+"(&!!,X)(&!!),Y&!!,X "
290   mne$=mne$+"&!! (&!!!!)&!!,Y "
300   $tables%=mne$:tables%=tables%+256
310   REM *** opcode and addressing data ***
320   DATA 16,39,16,16,16,35,35,16,16,36
```

```
330   DATA 17,16,16,50,50,16,42,40,16,16
340   DATA 16,41,39,16,16,54,16,16,16,53
350   DATA 53,16,50,39,16,16,35,35,35,16
360   DATA 16,36,17,16,50,50,50,16,42,40
370   DATA 16,16,16,41,41,16,16,54,16,16
380   DATA 16,53,53,16,16,39,16,16,16,35
390   DATA 35,16,16,36,17,16,50,50,50,16
400   DATA 42,40,16,16,16,41,41,16,16,54
410   DATA 16,16,16,53,53,16,16,39,16,16
420   DATA 16,35,35,16,16,36,16,16,17,59
430   DATA 50,16,42,40,16,16,16,41,16,16
440   DATA 16,54,16,16,16,53,16,16,16,39
450   DATA 16,16,35,35,35,16,16,16,16,16
460   DATA 50,50,50,16,42,40,16,16,41,41
470   DATA 44,16,16,54,16,16,16,53,16,16
480   DATA 36,39,36,16,35,35,35,16,16,36
490   DATA 16,16,50,50,50,16,42,40,16,16
500   DATA 41,41,44,16,16,54,16,16,53,53
510   DATA 54,16,36,39,16,16,35,35,35,16
520   DATA 16,36,16,16,50,50,50,16,42,40
530   DATA 16,16,16,41,41,16,16,54,16,16
540   DATA 16,53,53,16,36,39,16,16,35,35
550   DATA 35,16,16,36,16,16,50,50,50,16
560   DATA 42,40,16,16,16,41,41,16,16,54
570   DATA 16,16,16,53,53,16
580   FOR read%=0 TO 255
590     READ code%
600     tables%?read%=code%
610     NEXT
620   DATA &1E,&66,&A8,&A8,&A8,&66,&06
630   DATA &A8,&6C,&66,&06,&A8,&A8,&66
640   DATA &06,&A8,&1B,&66,&A8,&A8,&A8
650   DATA &66,&06,&A8,&27,&66,&A8,&A8
```

```
660    DATA &A8,&66,&06,&A8,&54,&03,&A8
670    DATA &A8,&12,&03,&75,&A8,&72,&03
680    DATA &75,&A8,&12,&03,&75,&A8,&15
690    DATA &03,&A8,&A8,&A8,&03,&75,&A8
700    DATA &84,&03,&A8,&A8,&A8,&03,&75
710    DATA &A8,&7B,&45,&A8,&A8,&A8,&45
720    DATA &60,&A8,&69,&45,&60,&A8,&51
730    DATA &45,&60,&A8,&21,&45,&A8,&A8
740    DATA &A8,&45,&60,&A8,&2D,&45,&A8
750    DATA &A8,&A8,&45,&60,&A8,&7E,&00
760    DATA &A8,&A8,&A8,&00,&78,&A8,&6F
770    DATA &00,&78,&A8,&51,&00,&78,&A8
780    DATA &24,&00,&A8,&A8,&A8,&00,&A8
790    DATA &A8,&8A,&00,&A8,&A8,&A8,&00
800    DATA &A8,&A8,&A8,&8D,&A8,&A8,&93
810    DATA &8D,&90,&A8,&42,&A8,&9F,&A8
820    DATA &93,&8D,&90,&A8,&09,&8D,&A8
830    DATA &A8,&93,&8D,&90,&A8,&A5,&8D
840    DATA &A2,&A8,&A8,&8D,&A8,&A8,&5D
850    DATA &57,&5A,&A8,&5D,&57,&5A,&A8
860    DATA &99,&57,&96,&A8,&5D,&57,&5A
870    DATA &A8,&0C,&57,&A8,&A8,&5D,&57
880    DATA &5A,&A8,&30,&57,&9C,&A8,&5D
890    DATA &57,&5A,&A8,&39,&33,&A8,&A8
900    DATA &39,&33,&3C,&A8,&4E,&33,&3F
910    DATA &A8,&33,&39,&3C,&A8,&18,&33
920    DATA &A8,&A8,&A8,&33,&3C,&A8,&2A
930    DATA &33,&A8,&A8,&A8,&33,&3C,&A8
940    DATA &36,&81,&A8,&A8,&36,&81,&48
950    DATA &A8,&4B,&81,&63,&A8,&36,&81
960    DATA &48,&A8,&0F,&81,&A8,&A8,&A8
970    DATA &81,&48,&A8,&87,&81,&A8,&A8
980    DATA &A8,&81,&48,&A8
```

```
 990    tables%=tables%+256
1000    FOR read%=0 TO 255
1010      READ offset%
1020      tables%?read%=offset%
1030      NEXT read%
1040    REM ** set tab values 1,3 and 6 **
1050    tables%!256=&10306
1060    FOR pass=0 TO 2 STEP 2
1070      P%=tables%+&103
1080      [OPT pass
1090      .start
1100      LDA #&0E              / paged mode on
1110      JSR oswrch
1120      LDY #&00             / clear Y register
1130      STY address          / and low byte
1140      .loop
1150      LDA #32              / print two spaces
1160      JSR oswrch
1170      JSR oswrch
1180      LDX address+1        / put high byte in X
1190      LDY index            / and index in Y
1200      LDA (address),Y      / get opcode byte
1210      TAY                  / move into Y
1220      JSR disasemble
1230      LDA &EC              / see if key pressed
1240      CMP #&F0             / was it ESCAPE?
1250      BNE continue         / no, carry on
1260      JMP exit             / yes, finish
1270      .continue
1280      LDA index            / get index
1290      ADC no_bytes         / add number of bytes
1300      STA index            / save new index
1310      BCC loop             / branch if no carry
```

1320	INC address+1	/ else update high byte
1330	BCS loop	
1340		/ disassembly routine
1350	.disasemble	
1360	LDA tables%,Y	/ get mnemonic pointer
1370	STA &75	/ save it
1380	LDA tables%−256,Y	/ get coded byte
1390	TAX	/ save in X
1400	AND #&0F	/ mask off high nibble
1410	STA addr_mode	/ and preserve it
1420	TXA	/ restore coded byte
1430	AND #&F0	/ get number of bytes
1440	LSR A	/ rotate right four times
1450	LSR A	
1460	LSR A	
1470	LSR A	
1480	STA no_bytes	/ save result
1490	LDA #ASC"&"	/ print hex symbol
1500	JSR oswrch	
1510	LDA address+1	/ print high byte address
1520	JSR hex_print	
1530	LDA index	/ print low byte address
1540	JSR hex_print	
1550	LDA #32	/ print two spaces
1560	JSR oswrch	
1570	JSR oswrch	
1580	TYA	/ restore opcode
1590	JSR hex_print	/ and print it
1600	LDA #32	/ print a space
1610	JSR oswrch	
1620	LDY index	/ get index
1630	INY	/ increment it
1640	LDX no_bytes	/ get number of operands

```
1650    DEX                         / decrement it
1660    BEQ tab_characters          / branch if none to do
1670    LDA (address),Y             / get operand
1680    STA operand_low             / save it
1690    JSR hex_print               / print it
1700    LDA #32                     / print a space
1710    JSRoswrch
1720    DEX                         / decrement operand count
1730    BEQ tab_characters          / branch if none to do
1740    INY                         / else increment index
1750    LDA (address),Y             / and get next byte
1760    STA operand_high            / save it
1770    JSR hex_print               / and print it
1780    .tab_characters
1790    LDX no_bytes                / get bytes
1800    DEX                         / decrement number
1810    LDY tables%+256,X           / tab value
1820    LDA #&20                    / print space
1830    JSR oswrch
1840    .tab_space
1850    JSR oswrch
1860    DEY                         / decrement tab count
1870    BNE tab_space               / repeat until done
1880    LDY #&03                    / 3 characters to print
1890    LDX pointer                 / get pointer to mnemonics
1900    .mne_print
1910    LDA tables%-&200,X          / get ASCII code
1920    JSR oswrch                  / print it
1930    INX                         / increment pointer
1940    DEY                         / decrement character count
1950    BNE mne_print               / continue until done
1960    LDA #&20                    / print space
1970    JSR oswrch
```

1980	LDA addr_mode	/ get address mode code
1990	BEQ exit	/ if zero, no mode
2000	ROL A	/ calculate offset
2010	ROL A	
2020	ROL A	
2030	SEC	/ set carry
2040	SBC addr_mode	/ subtract code
2050	TAX	/ move into X
2060	LDA addr_mode	/ restore address mode code
2070	CMP #&0A	/ was it relative?
2080	BNE not_relative	/ no, branch
2090	CLC	/ yes, clear carry
2100	LDA index	/ get index
2110	ADC #&02	/ add two
2120	ADC operand_low	/ add to operand low
2130	STA operand_low	/ save result there
2140	.not_relative	
2150	LDY #&07	/ 7 bytes to do
2160	.mode_loop	
2170	LDA tables%−&15C,X	/ get address format byte
2180	CMP #ASC"!"	/ was it '!'?
2190	BNE no_pling	/ no, so branch
2200	LDA no_bytes	/ yes, replace. Get bytes
2210	CMP #2	/ is it two?
2220	BEQ two_bytes	/ yes, branch
2230	LDA operand_high	/ get high byte
2240	JSR hex_print	/ print over!
2250	LDA operand_low	/ get low byte
2260	JSR hex_print	/ print over!
2270	INX : INX : INX	/ add three to offset
2280	DEY : DEY : DEY	/ subtract 3 from count
2290	JMP three_bytes	/ bypass two
2300	.two_bytes	

```
2310    LDA operand_low         / get operand
2320    JSR hex_print           / print over!
2330    INX                     / update offset
2340    DEY                     / decrement count
2350    JMP three_bytes         / bypass two
2360    .no_pling
2370    JSR oswrch              / print address mode
                                  character
2380    .three_bytes
2390    INX                     / increment offset
2400    DEY                     / decrement count
2410    BNE mode_loop           / repeat until count = 0
2420    .exit
2430    JSR osnewl              / print RETURN
2440    RTS
2450    .hex_print
2460    PHA
2470    LSR A : LSR A
2480    LSR A : LSR A
2490    JSR FIRST
2500    PLA
2510    .FIRST
2520    AND#15 : CMP #10
2530    BCC over
2540    ADC#6
2550    .over
2560    ADC#48
2570    JMP oswrch
2580    ]
2590    NEXT
2600  PRINT"Machine Code assembled"
2610  INPUT"start address : &"ADDR$
2620  ADDR$="&"+ADDR$
2630  ADDR%=EVAL(ADDR$)
```

```
2640    address?1=ADDR% DIV 256
2650    ?index=ADDR% MOD 256
2660    !no_bytes=0
2670    CLS
2680    PRINT" *** MACHINE CODE DISASSEMBLER ***"
2690    PRINT
2700    PRINT CHR$(129);"address opcode mnemonics"
2710    PRINT TAB(0,23);
2720    PRINT CHR$(129);"press SHIFT to continue listing";
2730    VDU28,0,22,39,3
2740    *KEY0   CALL start || M
2750    CALL start
2760    END
```

14   ROM Copier

This final utility program will copy any 8K block of paged sideways memory. This is particularly useful with the advent of numerous sideways ROM/RAM boards that allow the user to store programs permanently in non-volatile RAM or EPROMs ready for down-loading into the normal RAM area. Programs may be written in BASIC or machine code—the ROM Copier makes no distinction.

Before turning to the program we should look at four important memory locations associated with the paged ROM/RAM area sited from &8000 to &9FFF inclusive.

> &FE30 : ROM select Register

This byte is located within the Sheila area of the MOS and it is used by the MOS to determine which of the paged sockets is currently in use.

The MOS has been designed to allow up to 16 sideways ROMs to be implemented, though only 4 are available for use on the BBC Micro's board, and the ROM chosen is selected by the bit pattern in the lower 4 bits of this register. The highest priority ROM is numbered 15 (00001111) and will normally be BASIC. This ROM socket is the rightmost on the printed circuit board (looking from the front).

> &F4 : Select Register Copy Byte

This location within zero page contains a RAM copy of the value held in the ROM select register.

> &F5 and &F6 : Paged ROM Addressing Vector

These two bytes act as a vector, holding an address pointer into a paged ROM.

Program 29

```
10    INPUT "Please input ROM socket number :"rom%
20    rom_memory=&70
30    source_rom=&72
40    FOR PASS=0 TO 3 STEP3
50        P%=&7BA0
60        [OPT PASS
70        .rom_copier
80        LDA #&2000 MOD 256        / seed relocation address
90        STA rom_memory
100       LDA #&2000 DIV 256        / which is &2000
110       STA rom_memory+1
120       LDA #&8000 MOD 256        / seed paged ROM address
130       STA source_rom           / which is &8000
140       LDA #&8000 DIV 256
150       STA source_rom+1
160       .loop
170       LDA source_rom           / seed MOS workspace
180       STA &F6                  / with start address
190       LDA source_rom+1         / of paged ROM
200       STA &F7
210       LDY #rom%                / get ROM number
220       LDX &F4                  / save current number
230       STY&F4                   / replace with number to be
                                       copied
240       STY &FE30                / inform Shiela
250       LDY#0                    / initialize index
260       LDA(&F6),Y               / get byte from paged
                                       ROM/RAM
270       STX&F4                   / restore operating ROM
280       STX&FE30                 / usually BASIC
290       STA (rom_memory),Y       / copy byte into RAM
300       CLC                      / clear carry
310       LDA rom_memory           / get low byte
```

```
320    ADC #1                    / add one to it
330    STA rom_memory            / save result
340    LDA rom_memory+1          / get high byte
350    ADC #0                    / and add carry to it
360    STA rom_memory+1          / save result
370    CLC                       / clear carry
380    LDA source_rom            / get low byte
390    ADC #1                    / add one to it
400    STA source_rom            / save result
410    LDA source_rom+1          / get high byte
420    ADC #0                    / add carry to it
430    STA source_rom+1          / save result
440    CMP #12                   / all 12 pages done?
450    BNE loop                  / no, repeat loop
460    RTS
470    ]
480    NEXT
490    CALL rom_copier
```

Four bytes in the user area are required by the program to hold two vectored addresses. These two addresses point to the current address being accessed in the paged ROM (source_rom) and the area of RAM into which it will be copied. The relocation area for the copied memory is the 8K from &2000.

The program began by seeding the two vectors with their start addresses, &8000 and &2000 (lines 80 to 150). The source address is reflected also in the paged ROM addressing vector to keep the MOS happy (line 200). The previously input ROM socket value is in turn loaded into the ROM select vector and its RAM copy (lines 230 and 240). Note that its previous value is preserved in the X register (line 220).

Using the appropriate zero page vector, a byte is read from within the selected paged ROM (lines 250 and 260) and copied into RAM (line 290) after restoring the original ROM select values (lines 270 and 280). Lines 300 to 430 increment the values in the two vectors and the loop continues until all 12 memory pages have been copied (lines 440 and 450).

Appendix 1: Operating System Calls

Routine (name)	Address (hex)	Vector (hex)	Function	Register/s involved
OSWRCH	FFEE	20E	Write character	A
OSRDCH	FFE0	210	Read character	A
OSNEWL	FFE7	—	LF and CR to screen	A
OSASCI	FFE3	—	Write character (NL if A = 0D)	A
OSCLI	FFF7	208	Interprets command line	X,Y
OSBYTE	FFF4	20A	All OSBYTE calls and *FX	A,X,Y
OSWORD	FFF1	20C	All OSWORD calls	A,X,Y
OSFILE	FFDD	212	Load and save file	A,X,Y
OSBGET	FFD7	216	Load and save data file	A,X,Y
OSBPUT	FFD4	218	Put byte in file	A,Y
OSFIND	FFCE	21C	Open or close file	A,X,Y
OSGBPB	FFD1	21A	Multiple OSBPUT and OSBGET	A,X,Y
NVRDCH	FFCB	—	Non-vectored read character	
NVWRCH	FFC8	—	Non-vectored write character	
GSREAD	FFC5	—	Read string character	
OSEVEN	FFBF	—	Activate event	
GSINIT	FFC2	—	Initialize string input	
OSRDRM	FFB9	—	Read paged ROM byte	

Appendix 2: 6502 Complete Instruction Set

ADC	Add with carry		NZCV
Address mode	*Op-code*	*Bytes*	*Cycles*
Immediate	&69	2	2
Zero page	&65	2	3
Zero page,X	&75	2	4
Absolute	&6D	3	4
Absolute,X	&7D	3	4 or 5
Absolute,Y	&79	3	4 or 5
(Indirect,X)	&61	2	6
(Indirect),Y	&71	2	5

AND	AND with accumulator		NZ
Address mode	*Op-code*	*Bytes*	*Cycles*
Immediate	&29	2	2
Zero page	&25	2	3
Zero page,X	&35	2	4
Absolute	&2D	3	4
Absolute,X	&3D	3	4 or 5
Absolute,Y	&39	3	4 or 5
(Indirect,X)	&21	2	6
(Indirect),Y	&31	2	5

ASL   Shift left   NZC

Address mode	Op-code	Bytes	Cycles
Accumulator	&0A	1	2
Zero page	&06	2	5
Zero page,X	&16	2	6
Absolute	&0E	3	6
Absolute,X	&1E	3	7

BCC   Branch if C = 0   Flags unaltered

Address mode	Op-code	Bytes	Cycles
Relative	&90	2	3 or 2

BCS   Branch if C = 1   Flags unaltered

Address mode	Op-code	Bytes	Cycles
Relative	&B0	2	3 or 2

BEQ   Branch if Z = 1   Flags unaltered

Address mode	Op-code	Bytes	Cycles
Relative	&F0	2	3 or 2

BIT   Z,N,V

Address mode	Op-code	Bytes	Cycles
Zero page	&24	2	3
Absolute	&2C	3	4

BMI   Branch if N = 1   Flags unaltered

Address mode	Op-code	Bytes	Cycles
Relative	&3Ø	2	3 or 2

BNE   Branch if Z = Ø   Flags unaltered

Address mode	Op-code	Bytes	Cycles
Relative	&DØ	2	3 or 2

BPL   Branch if N = Ø   Flags unaltered

Address mode	Op-code	Bytes	Cycles
Relative	&1Ø	2	3 or 2

BRK   Break   B flag = 1

Address mode	Op-code	Bytes	Cycles
Implied	&00	1	7

BVC   Branch if V = 0   Flags unaltered

Address mode	Op-code	Bytes	Cycles
Relative	&50	2	3 or 2

BVS   Branch if V = 1   Flags unaltered

Address mode	Op-code	Bytes	Cycles
Relative	&70	2	3 or 2

CLC   Clear Carry flag   C flag = 0

Address mode	Op-code	Bytes	Cycles
Implied	&18	1	2

CLD   Clear Decimal flag   D flag = 0

Address mode	Op-code	Bytes	Cycles
Implied	&D8	1	2

CLI   Clear Interrupt flag   I flag = 0

Address mode	Op-code	Bytes	Cycles
Implied	&58	1	2

CLV   Clear Overflow flag   V flag = 0

Address mode	Op-code	Bytes	Cycles
Implied	&B8	1	2

CMP   Compare accumulator   NZC

Address mode	Op-code	Bytes	Cycles
Immediate	&C9	2	2
Zero page	&C5	2	3
Zero page,X	&D5	2	4
Absolute	&CD	3	4
Absolute,X	&DD	3	4 or 5
Absolute,Y	&D9	3	4 or 5
(Indirect,X)	&C1	2	6
(Indirect),Y	&D1	2	5 or 6

CPX   Compare X register   NZC

Address mode	Op-code	Bytes	Cycles
Immediate	&EØ	2	2
Zero page	&E4	2	3
Absolute	&EC	3	4

CPY   Compare Y register   NZC

Address mode	Op-code	Bytes	Cycles
Immediate	&CØ	2	2
Zero page	&C4	2	3
Absolute	&CC	3	4

DEC   Decrement memory   NZ

Address mode	Op-code	Bytes	Cycles
Zero page	&C6	2	5
Zero page,X	&D6	2	6
Absolute	&CE	3	6
Absolute,X	&DE	3	7

DEX   Decrement X register   NZ

Address mode	Op-code	Bytes	Cycles
Implied	&CA	1	2

DEY Decrement Y register NZ

Address mode	Op-code	Bytes	Cycles
Implied	&88	1	2

EOR Exclusive-OR NZ

Address mode	Op-code	Bytes	Cycles
Immediate	&49	2	2
Zero page	&45	2	3
Zero page,X	&55	2	4
Absolute	&4D	3	4
Absolute,X	&5D	3	4 or 5
Absolute,Y	&59	3	4 or 5
(Indirect,X)	&41	2	6
(Indirect),Y	&51	2	5

INC Increment memory NZ

Address mode	Op-code	Bytes	Cycles
Zero page	&E6	2	5
Zero page,X	&F6	2	6
Absolute	&EE	3	6
Absolute,X	&FE	3	7

INX   Increment X register   NZ

Address mode	Op-code	Bytes	Cycles
Implied	&E8	1	2

INY   Increment Y register   NZ

Address mode	Op-code	Bytes	Cycles
Implied	&C8	1	2

JMP   Jump   Flags unaltered

Address mode	Op-code	Bytes	Cycles
Absolute	&4C	3	3
Indirect	&6C	3	5

JSR   Jump to subroutine   Flags unaltered

Address mode	Op-code	Bytes	Cycles
Absolute	&20	3	6

LDA   Load accumulator   NZ

Address mode	Op-code	Bytes	Cycles
Immediate	&A9	2	2
Zero page	&A5	2	3
Zero page,X	&B5	2	4
Absolute	&AD	3	4
Absolute,X	&BD	3	4 or 5
Absolute,Y	&B9	3	4 or 5
(Indirect,X)	&A1	2	6
(Indirect),Y	&B1	2	5 or 6

LDX   Load X register   NZ

Address mode	Op-code	Bytes	Cycles
Immediate	&A2	2	2
Zero page	&A6	2	3
Zero page,Y	&B6	2	4
Absolute	&AE	3	4
Absolute,Y	&BE	3	4 or 5

LDY   Load Y register   NZ

Address mode	Op-code	Bytes	Cycles
Immediate	&AØ	2	2
Zero page	&A4	2	3
Zero page,X	&B4	2	4
Absolute	&AC	3	4
Absolute,X	&BC	3	4 or 5

LSR   Logical shift right   N = 0,ZC

Address mode	Op-code	Bytes	Cycles
Accumulator	&4A	1	2
Zero page	&46	2	5
Zero page,X	&56	2	6
Absolute	&4E	3	6
Absolute,X	&5E	3	7

NOP   No operation   Flags unaltered

Address mode	Op-code	Bytes	Cycles
Implied	&EA	1	2

ORA   Inclusive OR   NZ

Address mode	Op-code	Bytes	Cycles
Immediate	&09	2	2
Zero page	&05	2	3
Zero page,X	&15	2	4
Absolute	&0D	3	4
Absolute,X	&1D	3	4 or 5
Absolute,Y	&19	3	4 or 5
(Indirect,X)	&01	2	6
(Indirect),Y	&11	2	5

PHA   Push accumulator   Flags unaltered

Address mode	Op-code	Bytes	Cycles
Implied	&48	1	3

PHP   Push Status register   Flags unaltered

Address mode	Op-code	Bytes	Cycles
Implied	&08	1	3

PLA   Pull accumulator   NZ

Address mode	Op-code	Bytes	Cycles
Implied	&68	1	4

PLP   Pull Status register   Flags as status

Address mode	Op-code	Bytes	Cycles
Implied	&28	1	4

ROL   Rotate left   NZC

Address mode	Op-code	Bytes	Cycles
Accumulator	&2A	1	2
Zero page	&26	2	5
Zero page,X	&36	2	6
Absolute	&2E	3	6
Absolute,X	&3E	3	7

ROR   Rotate right   NZC

Address mode	Op-code	Bytes	Cycles
Accumulator	&6A	1	2
Zero page	&66	2	5
Zero page,X	&76	2	6
Absolute	&6E	3	6
Absolute,X	&7E	3	7

RTI   Return from interrupt   Flags as pulled

Address mode	Op-code	Bytes	Cycles
Implied	&40	1	6

RTS	Return from subroutine		Flags unaltered
Address mode	*Op-code*	*Bytes*	*Cycles*
Implied	&60	1	6

SBC	Subtract from accumulator		NZCV
Address mode	*Op-code*	*Bytes*	*Cycles*
Immediate	&E9	2	2
Zero page	&E5	2	3
Zero page,X	&F5	2	4
Absolute	&ED	3	4
Absolute,X	&FD	3	4 or 5
Absolute,Y	&F9	3	4 or 5
(Indirect,X)	&E1	2	6
(Indirect),Y	&F1	2	5 or 6

SEC	Set Carry flag		C = 1
Address mode	*Op-code*	*Bytes*	*Cycles*
Implied	&38	1	2

SED	Set Decimal flag		D = 1
Address mode	*Op-code*	*Bytes*	*Cycles*
Implied	&F8	1	2

SEI	Set Interrupt flag		$I = 1$
Address mode	*Op-code*	*Bytes*	*Cycles*
Implied	&78	1	2

STA	Store accumulator		Flags unaltered
Address mode	*Op-code*	*Bytes*	*Cycles*
Zero page	&85	2	3
Zero page,X	&95	2	4
Absolute	&8D	3	4
Absolute,X	&9D	3	5
Absolute,Y	&99	3	5
(Indirect,X)	&81	2	6
(Indirect),Y	&91	2	6

STX	Store X register		Flags unaltered
Address mode	*Op-code*	*Bytes*	*Cycles*
Zero page	&86	2	3
Zero page,Y	&96	2	4
Absolute	&8E	3	4

STY	Store Y register		Flags unaltered

Address mode	Op-code	Bytes	Cycles
Zero page	&84	2	3
Zero page,X	&94	2	4
Absolute	&8C	3	4

TAX	Transfer accumulator to X		NZ

Address mode	Op-code	Bytes	Cycles
Implied	&AA	1	2

TAY	Transfer accumulator to Y		NZ

Address mode	Op-code	Bytes	Cycles
Implied	&A8	1	2

TXA	Transfer X to accumulator		NZ

Address mode	Op-code	Bytes	Cycles
Implied	&8A	1	2

TYA	Transfer Y to accumulator		NZ
Address mode	*Op-code*	*Bytes*	*Cycles*
Implied	&98	1	2

TSX	Transfer Stack Pointer to X		NZ
Address mode	*Op-code*	*Bytes*	*Cycles*
Implied	&BA	1	2

TXS	Transfer X to Stack Pointer		Flags unaltered
Address mode	*Op-code*	*Bytes*	*Cycles*
Implied	&9A	1	2

Appendix 3: 6502 Opcodes

All numbers are hexadecimal.

00	BRK implied		1C	Future expansion
01	ORA (zero page, X)		1D	ORA absolute, X
02	Future expansion		1E	ASL absolute, X
03	Future expansion		1F	Future expansion
04	Future expansion		20	JSR absolute
05	ORA zero page		21	AND (zero page, X)
06	ASL zero page		22	Future expansion
07	Future expansion		23	Future expansion
08	PHP implied		24	BIT zero page
09	ORA #immediate		25	AND zero page
0A	ASL accumulator		26	ROL zero page
0B	Future expansion		27	Future expansion
0C	Future expansion		28	PLP implied
0D	ORA absolute		29	AND #immediate
0E	ASL absolute		2A	ROL accumulator
0F	Future expansion		2B	Future expansion
10	BPL relative		2C	BIT absolute
11	ORA (zero page), Y		2D	AND absolute
12	Future expansion		2E	ROL absolute
13	Future expansion		2F	Future expansion
14	Future expansion		30	BMI relative
15	ORA zero page, X		31	AND (zero page), Y
16	ASL zero page, X		32	Future expansion
17	Future expansion		33	Future expansion
18	CLC implied		34	Future expansion
19	ORA absolute, Y		35	AND zero page, X
1A	Future expansion		36	ROL zero page, X
1B	Future expansion		37	Future expansion

38	SEC implied	5D	EOR absolute, X
39	AND absolute, Y	5E	LSR absolute, X
3A	Future expansion	5F	Future expansion
3B	Future expansion	60	RTS implied
3C	Future expansion	61	ADC (zero page, X)
3D	AND absolute, X	62	Future expansion
3E	ROL absolute, X	63	Future expansion
3F	Future expansion	64	Future expansion
40	RTI implied	65	ADC zero page
41	EOR (zero page, X)	66	ROR zero page
42	Future expansion	67	Future expansion
43	Future expansion	68	PLA implied
44	Future expansion	69	ADC #immediate
45	EOR zero page	6A	ROR accumulator
46	LSR zero page	6B	Future expansion
47	Future expansion	6C	JMP (indirect)
48	PHA implied	6D	ADC absolute
49	EOR #immediate	6E	ROR absolute
4A	LSR accumulator	6F	Future expansion
4B	Future expansion	70	BVS relative
4C	JMP absolute	71	ADC (zero page), Y
4D	EOR absolute	72	Future expansion
4E	LSR absolute	73	Future expansion
4F	Future expansion	74	Future expansion
50	BVC relative	75	ADC zero page, X
51	EOR (zero page), Y	76	ROR zero page, X
52	Future expansion	77	Future expansion
53	Future expansion	78	SEI implied
54	Future expansion	79	ADC absolute, Y
55	EOR zero page, X	7A	Future expansion
56	LSR zero page, X	7B	Future expansion
57	Future expansion	7C	Future expansion
58	CLI implied	7D	ADC absolute, X
59	EOR absolute, Y	7E	ROR absolute, X
5A	Future expansion	7F	Future expansion
5B	Future expansion	80	Future expansion
5C	Future expansion	81	STA (zero page, X)

82	Future expansion	A7	Future expansion
83	Future expansion	A8	TAY implied
84	STY zero page	A9	LDA #immediate
85	STA zero page	AA	TAX implied
86	STX zero page	AB	Future expansion
87	Future expansion	AC	LDY absolute
88	**DEY implied**	AD	LDA absolute
89	Future expansion	AE	LDX absolute
8A	TXA implied	AF	Future expansion
8B	Future expansion	B0	BCS relative
8C	STY absolute	B1	LDA (zero page), Y
8D	STA absolute	B2	Future expansion
8E	STX absolute	B3	Future expansion
8F	Future expansion	B4	LDY zero page, X
90	BCC relative	B5	LDA zero page, X
91	STA (zero page), Y	B6	LDX zero page, Y
92	Future expansion	B7	Future expansion
93	Future expansion	B8	CLV implied
94	STY zero page, X	B9	LDA absolute, Y
95	STA zero page, X	BA	TSX implied
96	STX zero page, Y	BB	Future expansion
97	Future expansion	BC	LDY absolute, X
98	TYA implied	BD	LDA absolute, X
99	STA absolute, Y	BE	LDX absolute, Y
9A	TXS implied	BF	Future expansion
9B	Future expansion	C0	CPY #immediate
9C	Future expansion	C1	CMP (zero page, X)
9D	STA absolute, X	C2	Future expansion
9E	Future expansion	C3	Future expansion
9F	Future expansion	C4	CPY zero page
A0	LDY #immediate	C5	CMP zero page
A1	LDA (zero page, X)	C6	DEC zero page
A2	LDX #immediate	C7	Future expansion
A3	Future expansion	C8	INY implied
A4	LDY zero page	C9	CMP #immediate
A5	LDA zero page	CA	DEX implied
A6	LDX zero page	CB	Future expansion

158

CC CPY absolute	E6 INC zero page
CD CMP absolute	E7 Future expansion
CE DEC absolute	E8 INX implied
CF Future expansion	E9 SBC #immediate
D0 BNE relative	EA NOP implied
D1 CMP (zero page), Y	EB Future expansion
D2 Future expansion	EC CPX absolute
D3 Future expansion	ED SBC absolute
D4 Future expansion	EE INC absolute
D5 CMP zero page, X	EF Future expansion
D6 DEC zero page, X	F0 BEQ relative
D7 Future expansion	F1 SBC (zero page), Y
D8 CLD implied	F2 Future expansion
D9 CMP absolute, Y	F3 Future expansion
DA Future expansion	F4 Future expansion
DB Future expansion	F5 SBC zero page, X
DC Future expansion	F6 INC zero page, X
DD CMP absolute, X	F7 Future expansion
DE DEC absolute, X	F8 SED implied
DF Future expansion	F9 SBC absolute, Y
E0 CPX #immediate	FA Future expansion
E1 SBC (zero page, X)	FB Future expansion
E2 Future expansion	FC Future expansion
E3 Future expansion	FD SBC absolute, X
E4 CPX zero page	FE INC absolute, X
E5 SBC zero page	FF Future expansion

Appendix 4: ASCII Codes

The 'American Standard Code for Information Interchange' (no wonder it's shortened to ASCII!), is used by virtually all microcomputers as a way of coding letters and a range of 'control characters' so that they may be handled by number conscious micros.

The ASCII codes 0–31 are known as the control codes. Table A4.1 summarizes each one. You may well recognize these as the VDU commands, because that is exactly what they are!

Table A4.1

Decimal	Hex	Abbreviation	Meaning
0	0	NUL	Do nothing!
1	1	SOH	Reserved
2	2	STX	Reserved
3	3	ETX	Reserved
4	4	EOT	Write text at cursor
5	5	ENQ	Write text at graphics cursor
6	6	ACK	Enable ASCII codes
7	7	BEL	Bleep internal speaker
8	8	BS	Move text cursor back a single space
9	9	HT	Move text cursor forward a single space
10	A	LF	Line feed
11	B	VT	Vertical tab (move up a single line)
12	C	FF	Clear text area
13	D	CR	Carriage return (cursor to start of line)
14	E	SO	Paged mode on
15	F	SI	Paged mode off
16	10	DLE	Clear graphics area
17	11	DC1	Define text colour
18	12	DC2	Define graphics colour—expects two extra bytes to follow
19	13	DC3	Define logical colour—expects five extra bytes to follow
20	14	DC4	Restore default logical colours
21	15	NAK	Disable ASCII codes or delete current line
22	16	SYN	Select screen mode
23	17	ETB	Define character
24	18	CAN	Define graphics window
25	19	EM	PLOT K, X, Y
26	1A	SUB	Restore default windows
27	1B	ESC	ESCAPE
28	1C	FS	Define text window
29	1D	GS	Define graphics origin
30	1E	RS	Home cursor to top left of screen
31	1F	US	TAB X, Y

The numbers 32–127 are used to define letters, numbers and punctuation marks, and are detailed in Table A4.2. When the Beeb is using ASCII data it passes it through to the OSWRCH or OSASCI routines which treat it as such, rather than as hex data.

Table A4.2

Decimal	Hex	ASCII	Decimal	Hex	ASCII
32	20	(space)	81	51	Q
33	21	!	82	52	R
34	22	"	83	53	S
35	23	#	84	54	T
36	24	$	85	55	U
37	25	%	86	56	V
38	26	&	87	57	W
39	27	'	88	58	X
40	28	(	89	59	Y
41	29	)	90	5A	Z
42	2A	*	91	5B	[
43	2B	+	92	5C	\
44	2C	,	93	5D	]
45	2D	−	94	5E	^
46	2E	.	95	5F	−
47	2F	/	96	60	`
48	30	0	97	61	a
49	31	1	98	62	b
50	32	2	99	63	c
51	33	3	100	64	d
52	34	4	101	65	e
53	35	5	102	66	f
54	36	6	103	67	g
55	37	7	104	68	h
56	38	8	105	69	i
57	39	9	106	6A	j
58	3A	:	107	6B	k
59	3B	;	108	6C	l
60	3C	<	109	6D	m
61	3D	=	110	6E	n
62	3E	>	111	6F	o
63	3F	?	112	70	p
64	40	@	113	71	q
65	41	A	114	72	r
66	42	B	115	73	s
67	43	C	116	74	t
68	44	D	117	75	u
69	45	E	118	76	v
70	46	F	119	77	w
71	47	G	120	78	x
72	48	H	121	79	y
73	49	I	122	7A	z
74	4A	J	123	7B	(
75	4B	K	124	7C	¦
76	4C	L	125	7D	)
77	4D	M	126	7E	~
78	4E	N	127	7F	delete
79	4F	O	128	80	
80	50	P	129	81	

Index

Other titles of interest

Easy Programming for the BBC Micro   **£5.95**
Eric Deeson
'Probably the best elementary BBC Basic text.
An exceptionally readable book'—*BBC Micro User*.

Further Programming for the BBC Micro   **£5.95**
Alan Thomas
'If you are sinking with BASIC on your BBC Micro,
this could be your life raft'—*Education Equipment*.

Gateway to Computing with the BBC Micro   **hardback**
Ian Stewart   **(each) £6.95**
There are two books in the Gateway series
written especially for the BBC Micro. You'll be
learning and laughing in this new 'fun'   **paperback**
approach to computing.   **(each) £4.95**

BBC Micro Workshop Manual   **£6.95**
Bruce Smith
A helpful reference on many aspects of the
Beeb's hardware and software, designed for the
more advanced programmer.

BBC Micro Assembly Language   **£7.95**
Bruce Smith
'This book is the most readable of the several
covering the topic'—*Education Equipment*.

BBC Micro Utilities   **£6.95**
Bruce Smith
The BBC Micro Utilities package, of tape and
booklet will help the user overcome the first
hurdles of machine code programming.

Shiva publish a wide range of books for the BBC Micro, Electron, ZX Spectrum, Atari,
Dragon 32, VIC 20, Commodore 64, Commodore 16, Oric and Atmos computers, plus
educational games programs for the BBC Micro. Please complete the order form
overpage to receive further details.

ORDER FORM

I should like to order the following Shiva titles:

Qty	Title		ISBN	Price
_____	EASY PROGRAMMING FOR THE BBC MICRO		0 906812 21 6	£5.95
_____	FURTHER PROGRAMMING FOR THE BBC MICRO		0 906812 20 8	£5.95
	GATEWAY TO COMPUTING WITH THE BBC MICRO			
_____	BOOK ONE	hardback	1 85014 054 5	£6.95
_____	BOOK ONE	paperback	1 85014 034 0	£4.95
_____	BOOK TWO	hardback	1 85014 058 8	£6.95
_____	BOOK TWO	paperback	1 85014 038 3	£4.95
_____	BBC MICRO WORKSHOP MANUAL		1 85014 044 8	£6.95
_____	BBC MICRO ASSEMBLY LANGUAGE		0 906812 47 X	£7.95
_____	BBC MICRO UTILITIES		0 906812 65 8	£6.95
_____	....		....	.....
_____	....		....	.....
_____	....		....	.....

Please send me a full catalogue of computer books and software: ☐

Name ....

Address ....

....

....

This form should be taken to your local bookshop or computer store. In case of difficulty, write to Shiva Publishing Ltd, Freepost, 64 Welsh Row, Nantwich, Cheshire CW5 5BR, enclosing a cheque for £ ....

For payment by credit card: Access/Barclaycard/Visa/American Express

Card No .... Signature ....